D1161209

A Spanish Curse

or him that stealeth a Book from this
Library, let it change into a serpent in
his hand & rend him. Let him be struck
with Palsy, & all his Members blasted.
Let him languish in Pain crying aloud
for Mercy, let there be no surcease to his
Agony till he sink into Dissolution. Let
Bookworms gnaw his Entrails in token of
the Worm that dieth not, & when he goeth to
his final Punishment, let the flames of Hell
consume him for ever & aye.

Monastery of San Pedro
Barcelona

Library and archives conservation:
1980s and beyond

GEORGE MARTIN CUNHA
and
DOROTHY GRANT CUNHA

assisted by
Suzanne Elizabeth Henderson

Volume I

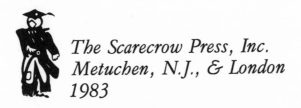
The Scarecrow Press, Inc.
Metuchen, N.J., & London
1983

This book has been printed
on permanent/durable paper
with a neutral pH to insure
a life expectancy of at least
one hundred years.

EARLHAM COLLEGE

OCT 4 1983

LIBRARY

Library of Congress Cataloging in Publication Data

Cunha, George Daniel Martin.
  Library and archives conservation.

    Vol. 2 has title: Bibliography.
    "A supplement to ... Conservation of library
  materials"--Vol. 2, introd.
    Includes indexes.
    1. Library materials--Conservation and restoration.
  2. Archival resources--Conservation and restoration.
  I. Cunha, Dorothy Grant. II. Henderson, Suzanne
  Elizabeth. III. Title.
  Z701.C784 1982   025.8'4   82-10806
  ISBN 0-8108-1587-7

TO PROFESSOR JOSEPHINE RISS FANG

Graduate School of Library and Information Science

Simmons College

Thus says the Lord of hosts, the God of Israel:

Take these deeds, both this sealed deed of
purchase and this open deed, and put them in
an earthenware vessel, that they may last for
a long time.

--Jeremiah 32:14

Oxford Annotated Bible 1977

TABLE OF CONTENTS

Appendices

ILLUSTRATIONS

Frontispiece: A Spanish Curse

FOREWORD

In November, 1981, it was my honor to speak before the
Twenty-Seventh Allerton Park Institute at the University of
Illinois, at Urbana-Champaign. I delivered the keynote
speech on the theme of conservation of library materials.
My comments largely dealt with two concerns that, after
working over a decade in preservation as a library manager
and administrator, I felt were central issues in preservation.
First, the library and archives professions cannot afford to
wait for the professional conservator to appear before taking up
the battle against decay: we must organize to take action
ourselves. The second is that preservation is a complex
and challenging problem, requiring the library profession to
develop its best critical judgment in dealing with preservation
in the broadest of collection development contexts. Restated
in a somewhat different way, preservation is another major
facet of sound management.

George and Dorothy Cunha have been saying that for
a long time.

My first personal contact with George Cunha was in
1971, when I attended a preservation workshop, sponsored
by the Texas Books Arts Guild at Southern Methodist University. Then Head of Special Collections Cataloging at the
Humanities Research Center at the University of Texas at
Austin, I had known the 1967 Scarecrow Press edition of
Conservation of Library Materials for several years. Cunha's
workshop, for a newcomer to the field, was a rich opportunity to see demonstrated many of the principles and practices
of his book. But of perhaps greater importance, I was infected with the missionary spirit, with which Cunha has
touched so many others over the years.

Well over a decade has passed since the first edition
of the 1967 work. In the years since, preservation has
moved from the concern of a few in a handful of institutions,
to a major interest of the library and archival professions.
Indeed, as a person who in the past three years has attempted

to chronicle developments in preservation for the ALA Yearbook, I am most impressed with the growing national momentum in preservation. This is manifested in grass-roots activities on the local level, in state and regional programs,
and in a number of significant major activities. I believe it
is a fair judgment to say that the forerunner of this book,
the earlier Conservation of Library Materials, was an important influence in these developments. Directed to libraries
and archivists, it provided a basic understanding of preservation components. The book became a bible to many who were
beginning to pick their way through the prickly thorns of preservation.

    With Carolyn Horton's excellent Cleaning and preserving
bindings and related materials, which appeared in that same
year, professionals beginning to address their preservation
needs felt that practical, usable information was being made
available to them, perhaps for the first time. The common
sense approaches of Cunha and Horton, as opposed to the
technically arcane nature of other specialized preservation
works, opened the door to many newcomers. These people--
these converts, if I can so characterize their enthusiasm and
sense of mission--became the cadre which worked to promote
the cause of preservation so broadly and so successfully in
the last decade. I should also add here that another factor
was the tireless efforts of George Cunha in speaking to scores,
perhaps hundreds, of groups in the past decade, exhorting
them to accept preservation as their responsibility, and to
begin to take action. In this, his contribution is unmatched.

    Because of the significant developments in the past
decade, many of which have brought about the formulation of
important new strategies and systems for dealing with preservation, another book is needed to set the stage for the next
decade. The Cunhas provide that with this work, which de-
scribes the most important influences and developments now
in place. Also, it looks to the future from a position which
addresses preservation from both a managerial as well as a
treatment perspective.

    That preservation is a component of a broad collection
development program cannot be overstressed. While individual items will continue to require the attention of professional
conservators working in treatment centers, the decisions of
what is to be treated, and what must be dealt with in other
ways will remain the responsibility of those managers and

administrators who direct our document depositories. This
book provides an invaluable look at the complex challenge
which that represents. Indeed, its authors have been instru-
mental in helping shape that very present and future that so
challenges us.

--Robert H. Patterson
The University of Tulsa

PREFACE

> ... as good almost kill a man as kill a good
> book: Who kills a man kills a reasonable crea-
> ture, God's image; but he who destroys a good
> book kills reason itself ...

--John Milton, <u>Areopagitica</u>, 1644

In his praise of books in the "speech for the liberty of un-
licensed printing" Milton was referring to censorship. In
his time book destruction by climate and light, chemical and
biological agents, and hard everyday use was of less concern
because books then were sturdy objects printed with carbon
ink on superb paper and with hand-sewn pages securely fastened to wooden or rope boards covered with long-lasting,
tough, durable leather. Seventeenth-century manuscripts
materials, prints, maps and broadsides were enduring to the
same degree.

If John Milton were alive today he would probably be
equally concerned by the continuing destruction of books by
the tens of millions because of the effects of the conditions
in most libraries today on books that all too often have been
made with inferior materials and by shoddy workmanship.
Today, libraries and archives are filled to bursting with books
and records, maps and broadsides, prints and pictures, audio-
visual materials, photographic prints and negatives, and
computer-generated records of our time that until recently
were regarded as foredoomed. In 1971 Frazer Poole, then
Assistant Director for Preservation at the Library of Congress,
predicted that by the year 2000 ninety percent of the books
then on library shelves would for various reason be beyond
salvage [7263]. We believe that because of the significant
developments in library conservation in the last ten years
Poole's dire prognostication will not happen. The reason is
that librarians, archivists, and others responsible for the cus-
tody of these records have accepted the challenge and are
now applying to this aspect of their work the good judgment,

professional ability, common sense and management skills that are characteristic of their profession.

The sum and substance of this book is: first, to provide an overview of some of the developments in the last fifteen years that are influencing conservation now; second, to provide broad general guidance on conservation management, preventive and restorative conservation, training and education, and disaster control; and third, to cautiously predict the future of this important aspect of librarianship. This volume with its bibliography of 5,871 citations is intended to be used in conjunction with our Conservation of Library Materials [7261] and the bibliography in Volume II of that book. The subject is now so vast and so much has happened in the last few years that complete coverage of library and archives conservation management and preservation techniques would require a multi-volume encyclopedia. This then is more "where to" than "how to" direction to use as a point of departure and general guide for conservation management. However, we have included in the text and appendices some specific "how to" instructions on matters we consider to be of particular importance.

As in our previous books we are indebted to many people for constructive criticism of our efforts. We hope that this volume will be accepted as a sincere effort to help librarians and archivists and others responsible for records to do their jobs. The list of those to whom we are obligated is much too long to present in its entirety. To list some of those who have helped would be an injustice to the others, but we must acknowledge the hundreds of hours of meticulous, painstaking work by our beloved daughter, Suzanne Henderson. Without her help this book would never have been completed. Any errors or shortcomings, however, are ours alone.

Lastly as in any rapidly developing field change is constant and every change will introduce new problems to be superimposed on the old. To keep things in perspective the reader should consider the following three axioms which are true not only for the information presented herein but are nearly universal in their application:

1. It is not that simple
2. It is not up to date
3. Someone, somewhere disagrees with it.

--GMC
--DGC

Chapter I

CONSERVATION TO 1980

The dramatic changes in the last two decades in the attitude of librarians and archivists toward conservation have been matched by an acceptance on the part of most professional conservators of the new role of others in the preservation of books and records. Twenty years ago all too many librarians were unaware of, or ignored, the alarming deterioration of books on their shelves and conservators seemed to think that they, alone, could handle the problems if they could get into the libraries and take charge. Slowly over the years custodians somewhat reluctantly perhaps, began to accept conservation as one of their management problems and conservators began to realize that the dimensions of the problem are such that by themselves they could never begin to do what has to be done.

In 1971 Frazer Poole, then Assistant Director for Preservation at the Library of Congress, reported that six million of the seventeen million books there were too brittle to use and that even to keep 10 percent of those six million in the national collection would cost eighteen million dollars and take thirty years to restore that 10 percent to usable condition.[1] It was about then that Mr. Poole predicted that almost all of the nonfiction published between 1900 and 1939 would be unusable by 1999. James Henderson, at that time Head of the Research Libraries, New York Public Library, had similar convictions about his collections and almost every library in this country was in the same situation. Figure 1 illustrates how the library profession had been overtaken by events in regard to conservation.

In the early 1970s book conservation began to emerge from a "dark age" of inability on the part of librarians to keep usable for even a brief time the ever-increasing number of newly published books which were being made with

Figure 1.

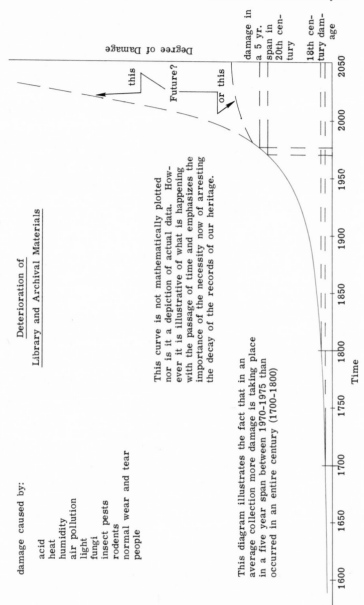

Deterioration of
Library and Archival Materials

damage caused by:

acid
heat
humidity
air pollution
light
fungi
insect pests
rodents
normal wear and tear
people

This curve is not mathematically plotted
nor is it a depiction of actual data. However it is illustrative of what is happening
with the passage of time and emphasizes the
importance of the necessity now of arresting
the decay of the records of our heritage.

This diagram illustrates the fact that in an
average collection more damage is taking place
in a five year span between 1970-1975 than
occurred in an entire century (1700-1800)

Degree of Damage

Future?

this

or this

damage in
a 5 yr.
span in
20th cen-
tury

18th cen-
tury dam-
age

Time

1600   1650   1700   1750   1800   1850   1900   1950   2000   2050

inferior materials and poor workmanship. Nor were they
able to properly care for the hundreds of millions of older
volumes in library stacks that were relentlessly being destroyed by unfavorable climates, dangerous lighting and acid
contamination. Regardless of Poole's gloomy forecast and
the conditions then prevailing in most libraries, we predicted in 1971 that all would not be chaos by the year 2000
because of the increasing awareness by librarians of this
unhappy situation and their increasing acceptance of the fact
that something had to be done. [2] Our prophecy is coming to
pass. Although all of the problems in regard to the preservation of library and archival materials have not been
solved, most have been identified and many of those still
unsolved are being aggressively investigated.

The Changing Trend

Cooperative conservation is firmly established in the Northeast and is recognized in other parts of the country as the
logical approach to the conservation of books and records.
Alternative means for mass deacidification of brittle books
at an acceptable cost will (in 1982) shortly be available.
Courses in conservation management and/or treatment techniques are being taught in most library schools. Trans-
cending all else is the realization by librarians and archivists and by professional conservators that the treatment of
collections in their entirety (rather than the treatment of
individual items) with emphasis on prevention of damage is
the most sensible approach to what has to be done.

The genesis was in the 1960s even before the 1966
Florence flood brought to the attention of the world at large
the problem of disasters in libraries. Florence, only one
of a long series of catastrophes large and small, was the
great catalyst in gaining support for some developments that
Sherelyn Ogden rightfully claims were already underway. [3]
The growing awareness by librarians of their book-care
problems during the preceeding three decades, the growing
interest by scientists in these problems, and the increasing
attention by professional conservators (who were in the beginning mostly museum oriented) were documented by Pamela
Darling and Sherelyn Ogden in 1980. [4] Their report is highly
recommended reading.

Unesco's International Centre for the Study of the
Preservation and Restoration of Cultural Property

(ICCROM) in 1968 in response to the growing worldwide cog-
nizance of the importance of the conservation of library materials organized an international seminar on that subject at
Rome's Istituto di Patologia del Libro.   Another milestone
was the 1969 conservation conference at the University of
Chicago.   The Chicago meeting, the first major gathering
at the university level of librarians, conservators, scientists, paper makers, and book publishers, resulted in the
publication of a volume[5] that will long be required reading
for all working in this field in any capacity.   The impetus
of the Chicago Conference continues today.

    The Temple University Law Library fire in 1973 and
the great conflagration at the St. Louis Federal Records
Center in the same year focused attention on disasters and
disaster control, including freeze stabilization of wet books
and freeze drying of frozen (stabilized) volumes, that resulted in major developments in these techniques (see Chapter VII).   The problem of mass deacidification of brittle
books, that was originally investigated at the W. J. Barrow
Research Laboratory, was picked up by Richard Smith with
financial support from the Public Archives of Canada and by
chemists in the Research Laboratory at the Library of Congress (see Chapter V).   In the 1970s there were in depth
studies of the effect of the environment, including temperature and humidity control, and the effect of natural and artificial lighting on books.   Paper chemists furthered the earlier studies of William J. Barrow and his associates at the
W. J. Barrow Research Laboratory in Richmond in the development of permanent/durable paper.

    Josephine Fang, as early as 1965, made conservation
required reading in her courses in library technical services
at the Simmons College School of Library Science.   Summer
courses in book conservation were first offered at the University of Illinois at Chicago Circle in 1971 under Paul
Banks' instruction.   Regularly scheduled courses during the
school year in conservation management, with credit towards
a degree in library science, began at the University of Rhode
Island's Library School in 1973 at about the same time that
similar courses for credit were offered at Wayne State University.   Both flourished and now almost every library
school in the country offers courses in conservation in their
annual catalogues--or are about to do so.

    In 1875 Justin Winsor at the Boston Public Library,
the first president of the American Library Association, was

acutely aware of the ever-increasing deterioration of book
paper and he wrote frequently on the subject as did Harry
Lydenburg at the New York Public Library in 1925.   Then
theirs were voices crying in the wilderness, but today there
is a flood of literature on the subject.   More and more of
this is being written by librarians who combine their expertise in other aspects of library science with knowledge
culled from conservators and scientific reports to formulate
realistic proposals for the solution of problems in book
care.   A significant number of major studies in conservation were supported in the 1970s by the American Library
Association, the Society of American Archivists, the Association of Research Libraries, and other library affiliated
alliances, usually with financial assistance from federal en-
dowments and private foundations.   As will be described in
Chapter II, they were important additions to the corpus of
information from other sources because most were investigations for librarians by librarians that are still having
much influence on general developments.

        Without the stimulus of public and private funding for
studies and actual conservation projects in the '70s, most of
the progress so far would not have been possible.   Conservation, even preventive conservation, is expensive--to suggest otherwise would be a deception.   Until they were dras-
tically curtailed in 1982 the National Endowment for the
Arts, the National Endowment for the Humanities and the
National Historical Publications and Records Commission
were generous in support of conservation programs.   The
Council on Library Resources, the Mellon Foundation, the
Rockefeller Foundation, and others in the private sector have
made possible projects for which public funding was unavail-
able.   The New England Document Conservation Center (now
the Northeast Document Conservation Center) was subsidized
for the first two years by the Council on Library Resources
matched by money raised by the New England Library Board,
the governing body for the Center.   The competition is great,
the funds available for grants limited, and the money goes
to those who best present their cases.   All too many worth-
while projects fail to gain grant support because the proposals are not well prepared.   Funding agencies have been
sympathetic to requests for assistance for teaching training
programs and for cooperative conservation efforts.   The
Foundation Directory lists sources of possible assistance,
particularly on the regional, state, or local level in addition
to the well-known federal agencies and major private foundations operating on a national level.   It might seem paradoxi-

cal that so much of the big agency money has gone to support programs in the larger and more affluent institutions
that are so much better off financially than so many others.
The big agencies do not particularly indulge these lucky establishments. Rather it is because the recipients work harder at it, do their homework better and often have full-time
fund raisers on their staffs who turn out a better product
(grant request). If any criticism of fund raising is warranted, it is that too much money seems to be going into
projects for feasibility studies and evaluations of the need
for conservation (reinventing the wheel)--money that could
be very well spent on teaching and training, establishing cooperative conservation efforts, and perhaps even getting
some preservation work done at the grassroots level.

Cooperation in Conservation

The early trend toward cooperative conservation resulted in
several successful centers for museum conservation, but so
far only one center for the conservation of library and archival materials. The events leading to cooperative conservation, reported in detail in the Pennsylvania Library
Association Bulletin, [6] are worth repeating. In Florence
March 12-14, 1970, the conference on International Cooperation for the Preservation of the Book, conducted by Unesco
and the Italian Ministry of Education, reviewed and discussed
the lessons learned from the Florence flood and the recovery
operation subsequently established in the Biblioteca Nazionale
Centrale. This meeting stressed the need for teaching and
training facilities to produce skilled personnel required for
the actual work on damaged books and also for the general
education of those in administrative and curatorial positions.
A proposal for the establishment of an international training
center was well received as were proposals regarding the
importance of centralizing and coordinating all preservation
activities for maximum effectiveness. A conference in
Copenhagen May 21-22, 1971 (Meeting of the Working Party
on the Physical Protection of Books and Documents), convened by the International Council on Archives, sought to
enhance cooperation at the international level between organizations and institutions concerned with the physical protection of books and documents. The conferees, among other
things, concluded that this problem required maximum cooperation between nations on the study of the physical protection of books and records, teaching and training in this
field, and in coordinating the efforts of all concerned toward

the most effective use of available resources.   It is important to note that in Florence and Copenhagen these facts were recognized and made a part of the record (see page 17).

Regional Centers

These four facts are the basis for the development of the regional centers for restoration conservation in the United States.   Science is developing techniques for successfully treating damage.   Practicing conservators, few as there are, are proficient in the application of these techniques. Unfortunately, the equipment and skills necessary for this work are expensive and their cost precludes the establishment of conservation workshops even in some of the largest libraries.   The rationale, therefore, for this aspect of cooperative library conservation is to establish strategically-located, professionally-operated, fully-equipped restoration centers to make available to all, at minimum cost, the highest quality repairs and restoration; training opportunities for conservation technicians; teaching facilities for the benefit of administrators and conservators; and paper laboratory and microreproduction facilities; all to encourage total conservation programs in the libraries, archives, public record depositories, and historical societies in a specified area.

The success in the museum field of the Intermuseum Conservation Association (ICA) at Oberlin, the first truly cooperative conservation effort in this country--which even before Florence and Copenhagen proved that the concept is sound--has been the motivation for other museum conservation centers throughout the country.   In 1972 the Government of Canada (The National Museum of Canada) created the Canadian Conservation Institute with a headquarters organization in Ottawa.   It is entirely conceivable that at some time in the future there could be similar support for Canadian libraries and archives, possibly within this organization.

The New England Document Conservation Center

In 1965 the Chief Conservator at the Library of the Boston Athenaeum, borrowing on the experience of the ICA, proposed the establishment of a Cooperative Library Conservation Association for New England and requested support for the idea from the New England Deposit Library (NEDL), a

cooperative with membership consisting of ten major libraries
in the Greater Boston area.   Meeting in January 1966, the
Trustees of NEDL agreed the idea had merit, but excused
themselves from participation because in their opinion the
idea "did not fall within the scope of their charter. "   The
idea was kept alive, however, by the Athenaeum's Director
and the Chief Conservator, both of whom took advantage of
every opportunity to speak and write on the subject.   At a
meeting of concerned records officers from five of the six
New England states in 1969 one of the agenda topics was the
difficulty and expense involved in arranging for the repair
of original documents.   The consensus was that there is
enough work to be done to justify the establishment of a
restoration laboratory in that part of the country and that
acting together the New England states might well support
such a project.

        The administrators of the New England Interstate Li-
brary Compact (a political subdivision of these six states),
when apprised of the situation in December 1969, resolved
to establish a conservation center "... to make available to
public libraries, state and local archival agencies and other
non-profit historical, educational, and cultural institutions
on a cooperative basis the means for preserving, repairing
and restoring important or unique documentary materials. "
Documentary materials in this sense include, in addition to
essential state and local records, books, prints, maps,
manuscripts, broadsides, and works of art on paper in the
collections of libraries, archives, historical societies, and
museums.   In January 1971 the Compact's administrators
submitted a proposal to the Council on Library Resources
for assistance in the establishment of a conservation center
patterned after that one proposed to the New England Deposit
Library by the Boston Athenaeum in 1965.   In November
1972 the Council approved a grant, thus enabling the administrators of the Interstate Library Compact to proceed in
that direction by the establishment on April 1, 1973 of the
New England Document Conservation Center.   Policy guidance
for this activity, authorized by the terms of a library agreement between the states and approved by the Attorney General of each state, was vested in a Board of Governors (the
State Librarian or counterpart in each state) which also ap-
pointed a Director charged with the operation of the Center.

        The objective of the Center is to administer and su-
pervise a workshop, necessary facilities, and staff to restore, preserve, and maintain the physical condition of books,

prints, maps, broadsides, manuscripts, and similar documentary materials of historic, archival, or cultural interest.
Whenever necessary for the accomplishment of those objectives, the Center will investigate materials and equipment
and conduct studies and tests in order to develop methods
to protect, preserve, and maintain the integrity or improve
the physical condition of such documentary materials; assist
member institutions to carry out conservation programs; and
render conservation services to them.   Funds originally required to establish the Center came from direct grants from
most of the New England states, foundation grants, and private contributions; all soon supplemented by revenues received for work done by the Center.   Now, in accordance
with the terms of its Charter, the Center is basically self-
supporting.

The Conservation Center located in Andover, Massachusetts, with its preservation workshops, teaching and
training facilities, photoduplication capabilities, and field
services, plus its staff of experts, is the first of its kind
anywhere.   Librarians, archivists, museum staffs, historical
society personnel, and public record administrators in New
York and New Jersey as well as the New England states
find in it practical solutions for their repair and restoration
requirements, guidance in preventive conservation, assistance
in emergencies, training of technicians and staff education in
the management aspects of conservation.

It is extremely important to realize that the first regional cooperative restoration center for library and archival
materials in the United States, the New England Document
Conservation Center[7] was established by librarians for the
benefit of libraries in general and not by scientists, practicing conservators, or commercially motivated interests to
"sell" their services to those in need of them.   The effect
of that precedent has been widespread.

Support from Regional Centers

The support that regional centers can provide is first and
foremost to be a clearing-house for conservation, a place
to turn to for answers to the multitude of questions that re-
peatedly arise in connection with the prevention of damage
and treatment after damage takes place.   If a regional center were never more than that, its existence would be justi-
fied.   Regional centers are the logical intermediary between

Figure 2.
THE TRIPARTITE CONCEPT OF CONSERVATION

Administration

Decision making based on all the
considerations involved in addition to the conservation factors.

Science

Study:

1. Causes for deterioration

2. Effect of the environment on
    materials

3. Chemical and physical char-
    acteristics of materials

Evaluate traditional procedures

Develop new procedures for
treatment of materials and
control of the environment

Establish staff policies
Plan and provide funds for con-
servation program
Emergency plans
Support regional cooperative con-
servation
Advocate the teaching of conserva-
tion in schools and colleges
Provide learning opportunities for
staff
Cooperate with scientists and pro-
fessional conservators
Support professional groups

Professional Conservation
Provide advice and assistance in:
1. Environment control
2. On the site treatments of
    materials
Teaching for institution staffs
Training for technicians
Establish standards
Conduct surveys and inspections
Conduct seminars and workshops
Perform sophisticated repairs
Disaster assistance

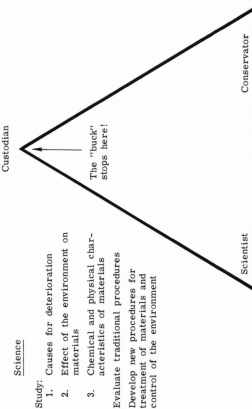

Custodian

The "buck"
stops here!

Scientist

Conservator

curators and administrators and the scientific community
and between the scientific community and professional conservators to provide a constant flow of reliable information
(see Figure 2).

Regional centers can provide the lecturers and in-
structors for the seminars and workshops that will be such
an important part of any preservation efforts in the years
to come. At regional conservation centers, when they become more than a clearinghouse for conservation (i. e. ,
provide workshop facilities staffed by conservators and conservation technicians), it will be possible for laymen to get
training in the simple cleaning, deacidification, mending and
reinforcing techniques for black and white flat paper and
simple book repairs that are the 80 percent of the work that
has to be done in libraries and which are legitimate "in-
house" preservation measures.

Regional centers can provide visiting professors for
courses in conservation and conservation administration at
schools of library science in the colleges and universities
that have such graduate programs.

Regional centers can provide conservators to do the
surveys of buildings and their collections that are such an
important early step in any conservation program.

Regional conservation centers will, of course, have
the necessary skills and sophisticated and expensive machinery and equipment to do that 20 percent of the repair
and restoration of collections that never should be attempted
in-house unless there is a professional conservator on the
staff.

Regional conservation centers can provide a microform service and processing facility for "preservation" microfilming, which is a thing apart from the commercial
services available (including so-called "archival" microfilming) and in some instances archival storage facilities, without which even the most expertly filmed and processed film
will not survive for the generations to come.

The Situation in 1980

As some of the earlier problems in library conservation had
been identified and solved, new problems emerged. In the

early 1970s acid was characterized as an "arch enemy" of
books which, if not brought under control, would result in
the total loss of untold millions of volumes because of the
embrittlement of their pages by acid contamination. In the
1980s when it appeared that techniques for the mass deacidification of books would help resolve the acid problem, we
learned that even though there may be no acid in paper (pH
7. 0 or above), there can be serious oxidative degradation of
the cellulose in book paper if a catalyst such as copper or
iron is present in even microscopic quantities. Recent investigations indicate that magnesium carbonate (a principle
deacidification agent) will control this oxidation to a certain
extent, and that treatment of paper with potassium iodide
will completely eliminate it.

Another example of the thoroughness of the investigations of the chemistry of paper that are taking place in the
laboratories are the reports by chemists at the Institute of
Book Pathology in Rome. They are now concerned that crystals of magnesium carbonate, which effectively neutralize
and buffer paper, damage the fibers of paper in which they
are enmeshed, thus reducing its folding strength (reduced
durability). These same chemists have indicated that these
studies so far indicate that the crystals of calcium carbonate, an equally good buffering agent, do not damage cellulose
fibers. When their studies are completed the formal report
of the investigation, when published, will undoubtedly result
in changes in treatment techniques.

To summarize--at long last in the 1980s, after a
period of almost complete indifference prior to 1960, a spell
of increasing awareness of the problems in the 1960s, then
a decade of study and investigation in the 1970s, librarians
and archivists are taking charge of conservation management
in their profession. The following chapters will describe
how that has come about.

References

1.   Poole, Frazer. "Thoughts on Conservation of Library
     Materials," in Library and Archives Conservation.
     Boston: Boston Athenaeum, 1972.

2.   Cunha, G. M. & D. G.   Conservation of Library Mate-
     rials Vol. 1.   Metuchen, N. J. : Scarecrow Press,
     1971 (see page 234).

3. Ogden, Sherelyn. "The Impact of the Florence Flood
    on Library Conservation in the United States of
    America," Restaurator 3:1-36, 1979.

4. Darling, Pamela and Sherelyn Ogden. "From Problems
    Perceived to Programs in Practice: The Preserva-
    tion of Library Resources in the U. S. A. 1956-80."
    Library Resources and Technical Services 25:9-29,
    Jan. 1981.

5. Winger, H. W. and R. D. Smith. Deterioration and
    Preservation of Library Materials. Chicago: Uni-
    versity of Chicago Press, 1970.

6. Cunha, G. M. "National Trends in Cooperative Ap-
    proaches to Conservation," PLA Bulletin 28(6):226-
    231, 1973.

7. Now the Northeast Document Conservation Center.

Chapter II

STUDIES INFLUENCING THE
DEVELOPMENT OF CONSERVATION

Most of what we know of conservation was gathered by
persons who were curious. If we relegate curiosity
to subordinate role, we shall sterilize accomplishments.
Comments about relevance and the solution of pressing
problems strike me as only a slight improvement over
the well known comment of a former Secretary of De-
fense that basic research is "when you don't know
what you're doing." It is only by accumulating facts
about a great diversity of things--most of them in-
significant in themselves--that we can begin to see
relationships and to find patterns that will guide us.
The realization that nothing less than knowledge must
be the goal of conservation does not frighten a curious
person, it merely stimulates him. What frightens him
is the difficulty of explaining why this must be so.

Paraphrased from observations by
Howard Evans in Life on a Little Known Planet

The sometimes abused proclivity of people to meet for the
discussion of mutual problems and an equal propensity for
studies of causes and effect have in the case of library and
archives conservation yielded a rich harvest. Many seminars and workshops on conservation in the last fifteen years,
combined with the results of pure research by scientists and
feasibility studies and development programs by conservators,
curators, and administrators of collections (plus the natural
desire to publish), have resulted in an abundance of printed
material from which those responsible for the care of collections can obtain guidance. Some of these published materials are of the utmost importance in regard to direction
for conservation policy. Many are reliable and articulate
texts for preventive conservation and repair and restoration
treatments. All are interesting.

In the following pages we comment on some of the published materials that, in our opinion, have influenced the development of library conservation to date and will effect future planning. What we have selected are by no means all of the significant studies and there will undoubtedly be those who disagree with our choice--so be it. For those who wish more information on these studies we suggest a perusal of the citations in the "general" category in each major section of the bibliography, Part II of this book.

Pioneer Work

John Murray's inquisitiveness about the causes for "the present state (1823) of that wretched compound called paper"[1] was matched by Edwin Sutermeister, a young chemist, at the S. D. Warren Paper Company mill. [2] Over a period of thirty years, beginning in 1901, he conclusively proved that the use of alkaline substances as fillers in the paper-making process could eliminate acid hydrolysis in paper, which he had identified as the principle cause for degradation early in his studies. William J. Barrow's work on the deacidification of books and documentary materials was influenced by Sutermeister's work.

Investigations for the last ten years have concentrated on the broader aspects of preventive conservation with emphasis on conservation management and the treatment of collections as a whole, rather than the treatment of individual objects. Examples are the mass deacidification studies completed at the W. J. Barrow Research Laboratory in Richmond before its work was terminated[3] and the similar studies rapidly nearing completion at the Library of Congress[4] and the archives of Canada. [5]

International Collaboration

At the cosmopolitan meeting in Florence in 1970, [6] the participants had great hopes for the establishment of an international center which librarians and conservators in all countries could turn to for help in all aspects of conservation. At the 1971 meeting in Copenhagen the representatives of the International Federation of Library Associations and the International Council on Archives discussed the physical protection of books and documents. [7] Both meetings were important, but subsequent attempts to follow up have not been

spectacular.   At both the Florence and Copenhagen meetings
the consensus was:

a)   Cooperative conservation is the key to the solution.
b)   Teaching and training is a major requirement at the
     beginning.
c)   Conservation is expensive.
d)   Centralization and coordination will help the costs.

These four assumptions have been the basis for many
of the studies that followed.   Useful fact-finding efforts were
those by Gay Walker, Yale University Libraries. [8, 9]   Walker's survey assembled data on: a) conservation educational
opportunities on the academic level and b) degree of deterioration of materials in academic libraries and corrective
action, if any, being taken.   Both revealed the casual attitude toward conservation prevailing at that time in most
academic libraries.   Based on her findings, Walker offered
for consideration a model preservation program to help improve the situation.

Nationwide Programs in the U. S.

In December 1976 a planning conference for a national preservation program was held in Washington. [10]   Presentations
and discussions by conservators, scientists, curatorial personnel, and administrators representing all categories of institutions delved into about every aspect of the problem.
The proceedings of the meeting have been evaluated by Ellen
McCrady[11] in comparison with the consensus in regard to
priorities reached at a conference at the University of Maryland in May 1980. [12]

By 1980 there was a National Preservation Program
Officer in the Library of Congress with an ad hoc Advisory
Committee to assist in establishing priorities and coordinating the implementation of the plan.   Progress toward these
national goals has been disappointing, although Pamela Darling has drawn attention to several significant advances[13]
that can be attributed to the 1976 idea.   They are public and
professional awareness, increased offering of preservation
topics in library school courses, the preservation institute
at Columbia University in 1978, the new program at Columbia for conservators and conservation administrators, and
increased publications on conservation.

The investigations by the National Conservation Advisory Council must be regarded as major contributions to conservation in general. [14]   The NCAC was established in 1973 to serve as a national forum for conservation interests by a) identifying major needs and problems and offering recommendations for their solution, b) recommending programs that would result in coordinated national policy and plans, and c) to consider the advisability of creating a national institute for conservation in the United States.   Each of the NCAC publications was prepared by committees of experts in the various aspects of conservation.   The Council's belief in the need for a national institute for conservation[15] does not yet have the unqualified support of all professional conservators but most of the differences of opinion that once prevailed between the various factions in the profession in regard to a national conservation institute seem to have been resolved when in April 1982 the NCAC, with the apparent acquiescence of the American Institute for Conservation, became the National Institute for the Conservation of Cultural Property, Inc.   See[16] and Chapter III, page 29.   Of particular importance to librarians and archivists are the NCAC's 1978 report on libraries and archives,[17] its report on regional centers,[18] and the Proceedings of the NCAC Regional Centers Seminar which was held in Oberlin, Ohio in February 1978.

Area Studies

An important study of the need for conservation facilities and services by Ohio Libraries, with conclusions that are indicative of the situation in almost all states, was done by Walter Brahm in 1977.[19]   In 1982 Brahm did a Midwest Regional Study for Materials Conservation with NEH support to identify those who have an interest and responsibility in the field, and invite their collaboration in the development of cooperative conservation in the Midwest.   The Commissioner of Libraries and Kentucky State Librarian in 1981 established a permanent conservation advisory committee to study the situation in Kentucky and develop long-range plans for establishments in the Commonwealth that have records of any sort pertaining to the political, social, cultural, and economic history of the area.

The July 1978 library conservation seminar at Rutgers University[20] is important because of the scope and caliber of the papers presented; the diverse backgrounds of the participants; its joint sponsorship by a chapter of the Special Libraries Association and the Library Binding Institute (representing business); and its financial support from the industrial firm E. R. Squibb & Sons. This is ample evidence of the across-the-board cooperation that has given momentum to conservation programs in some parts of the country.

The 1978 Institute on the Development and Administration of Programs for the Preservation of Library Materials at Columbia University was a landmark. [21] All of the fall outs were good, particularly the establishment of the program of education for conservation and conservation administration at Columbia University's School of Library Service (see page 39) and the new publication Conservation Administration News (CAN), a journal on conservation for librarians by librarians [10777].

The California Library Authority for Systems and Service (CLASS) 1979 publication, to call attention to a problem of national as well as state-wide concern, [22] was intended to be a blueprint for action in the conservation area leading to the creation of a California Conservation Center. Its analysis of the overall problem, and short and long range objectives are sound guidance for any state or regional program. Implementation state-wide has been slow compared to the work being done at the University of California campuses, such as the one at UC Berkeley. [23]

In April 1979, the University Libraries and the School of Library Science at the University of Oklahoma, together with the Oklahoma Department of Libraries convened a colloquium on preservation at the Oklahoma Center for Continuing Education in Norman. There were participants from most of the states west of the Mississippi River. [24] This meeting was unusual for two reasons. First, it was at long last a recognition in that part of the country that librarians in the West must face up to the problems of conservation. Second, in addition to the conventional presentations on organizing for conservation, preservative and restorative treatments for library materials, preservation of non-print materials (microforms), disaster and disaster prevention, there was a major challenge to all of these concepts by Wilfred Lancaster of the Graduate School of Library and Information Science, University of Illinois. He stated flatly that in the near future research libraries, as we know them today, as well as all of the associated technology would be replaced by computer data banks, even to the extent that it would not be necessary to have buildings to house books. Needless to say,

there was vehement discussion pro and con, all of which
emphasized the fact that machine readable records are becoming more and more part of the system.   To what degree
they will replace books--only the future will reveal.

Western States Materials Conservation Project

Howard Lowell's survey for the seventeen states Western
Council of Libraries[25] revealed that these states have virtually no conservation facilities and that administrators lack
elementary knowledge about conservation matters, proper
storage conditions, and disaster preparedness.   These were
the conclusions of the project staff and local participants
after planning conferences in each of the member states and
a final feasibility colloquium of representatives of public,
state, and university libraries, historical societies, archives,
and museums from all of the eighteen Western states at
Snowbird, Utah in June 1980.

        The WSMCP, in spite of some difficulties due to the
ambitious aims of the program and the huge geographic area
involved, was a success.   In return for a $96,000 investment
by the Western Council of State Libraries, Inc. and the National Historical Publications and Records Commission these
have been the results:

   a)   A survey report by the project staff identifying the li-
        brary and archives conservation needs in the West.
   b)   An aroused regional consciousness in regard to the
        conservation needs of libraries and archives in the
        West.
   c)   Fourteen states (out of seventeen particpating states)
        have embarked on conservation activities for which
        WSMCP can be identified as the catalyst.

        As the first part of a long-range objective to imple-
ment effective conservation practices in the Western U.S. ,
participants called for the creation of a regional conservation
clearinghouse.   An advisory group of the Western Council of
State Libraries, the sponsor of the Colloquium, was charged
with the development and establishment of the clearinghouse.
Some of the initial responsibilities of the clearinghouse were
to address needs for training and education within the region
and to initiate the formation of a conservation advocacy network.   Later stages of the master plan call for a collective
materials insurance pool, a master microfilm repository and
eventually for conservation laboratories.

Colloquium participants also formulated strong policy statements on the needs for a national conservation research program; publication of national standards; development of national, regional, state and local public policy; and legislation regarding conservation practices.

Recommendations for immediate actions included commissioning studies by the Western Council on specific aspects of the "state of the art" of conservation, establishing relationships with other relevant national groups like the Society of American Archivists and the American Library Association, and developing an advocacy network which could work toward the implementation of standards.

Specific recommendations for legislation included a suggestion that the Western Council should appoint a committee to draft a national conservation public policy statement which would support a wide range of funding efforts, in addition to those of the National Endowment for the Humanities and the National Historical Publications and Records Commission. Colloquium participants and the Western Council were also called upon to urge the adoption of uniform standards at state and local levels, and to pursue implementation of a new federal law requiring Library of Congress copyright copies to be submitted on durable, permanent paper.

Although Colloquium participants did not vote on the matter, there was informal consensus that the most effective conservation actions are those that can be implemented and funded at the local level. A shared concern throughout the meeting was that the master plan needed to be realistic and that parts of the plan should be designed so as to be possible for immediate implementation.

The University of California
Preservation Task Group

The Task Group on the Preservation of Library Materials, created by the University of California Library Council in July 1976, was directed to:

a) Determine the extent and rate of deterioration in the libraries' collections.
b) Study methods of preservation and conservation.
c) Recommend steps to slow the rate of deterioration and

recommend procedures to be followed in the event of disaster.

In its June 1977 report to the Library Council the Task Group[26] identified three "affordable" basic aspects of conservation.   They were: a) emphasis on prevention; b) the appointment of conservation librarians to supervise locally funded programs to cope with local problems; and c) the establishment of a conservation center (maybe two) to the UC library system.

The Task Group's more specific recommendations were in this vein:

a) Hire a professional conservator for six months for an objective study to assess the conservation requirements of all the libraries and do a feasibility study on the need for a conservation center.

b) Establish a new conservation officer position to organize and coordinate system-wide programs.

c) Formulate a comprehensive conservation/preservation policy statement for promulgation at each campus.

d) Each library formalize its commitment for conservation activities by creating permanently funded local programs.

e) Have a conservation librarian on each campus to coordinate preservation activities there and cooperate with the other conservation librarians in pooling of equipment, quality control, and other cost savings measures.

f) Adoption and implementation of environmental monitoring procedures.

g) Creation of sophisticated disaster plans.

This report was accepted by the library council, but implementation of the recommendations has been slow because of budget difficulties.   By early 1982 nothing had been accomplished on a system-wide basis; however, modest progress had been made on the campuses.   For instance the General Library of UC Berkeley had established a preservation office and UC Davis Library had a Department of Conservation.   In January 1982 with changes reflecting the Task Group's 1977 recommendations being written into the System-wide Master Plan, the Task Group members expect some positive results by 1983.

Committee on Production Guidelines

On May 14, 1979, at the invitation of representatives of the Andrew W. Mellon Foundation and the Council on Library Resources, nineteen individuals with knowledge of paper manufacturing, publishing, and book preservation programs met at the Century Association in New York City to exchange information about book paper, its use, and how to identify ways to address prospective aspects of the collection preservation problems that have been a matter of concern to librarians and scholars for many years. [27] Because of the large number of pertinent issues and their complex interrelation, the discussants concluded that there is need to expand understanding of the nature of the problem and to press for specific improvements as opportunities develop. At the conclusion of the discussion, those present encouraged the continued pursuit of issues identified during the preservation meeting. They formed a committee, under the direction of Herbert S. Bailey, Jr. of the Princeton University Press, to propose procedures for identifying objectives and options for action, to recommend ways to arrive at acceptable standards, and to extend understanding and wider recognition of the preservation problem itself.

This Committee on Production Guidelines for Book Longevity issued its first report[28] in April 1981. This important study should be read in its entirety by all librarians and used as policy guidance by all local, state, and regional library associations. The essence of the report is that economic conditions have increased interest by publishers in the production of acid-free book paper; it is not necessary that all books be printed on acid-free paper; publishers will have to make the decision as to which books should be printed on good paper, but they can be guided by professionals in the field and members of the scholarly community; that publishers identify acid-free books with an appropriate statement in each book; librarians must make publishers, including USGPO, aware of their needs; and publishers stock acid-free paper for use on appropriate titles.

Here is, at last, something relating to a meeting of the minds between publishers who must make money to stay in business and librarians who have to keep the publishers' products in usable condition anywhere from six to six hundred years. If industry and the library profession both accept the recommendations in this superb report, the impact on conservation in the generations to come will be profound.

References

1. The Gentleman's Magazine.   London 1823.

2. Brown, L. H.   Paper Permanence.   Boston: S. D. War-
    ren Paper Company, 1981.

3. Kusterer, J. E. and R. C. Sproull.   Gaseous Diffusion
    Paper Deacidification.   US Patent 3, 771, 958 No-
    vember 13, 1973 (the Morpholine Process).

4. Williams, J. C. and G. Kelly.   Method of Deacidifying
    Paper.   US Patent 3, 969, 599 July 13, 1976 (the
    Diethyl Zinc Process).

5. Smith, R. D.   "Progress in Mass Deacidification in the
    Public Archives," Canadian Library Journal 36(6):
    325-332 1979.   (The Magnesium Methyl Carbonate
    Process)

6. For a verbatim report of that meeting see the Bollettino
    dell'Istituto di Patologia del Libro 29(1-4) 1970.
    The entire issue.

7. Christiansen, P. A.   "Report of a Conference: Meeting
    of the Working Party on the Physical Protection of
    Books and Documents, Copenhagen May 21-22, 1971,"
    Restaurator 2(1):29-31, 1972.

8. Walker, G.   "Preservation Efforts in Larger U. S.
    Academic Libraries," College and Research Li-
    braries 36(1):39-44, Jan. 1975.

9. _____ .   Preservation Training and Information.
    Chicago: ALA Committee on the Preservation of
    Library Materials, Resources and Technical Serv-
    ices Division, 1976.

10. Proceeding of the Planning Conference for a National
    Preservation Program Held at the Library of Con-
    gress in Washington, D. C. on December 16 & 17,
    1970.   Washington: Library of Congress, 1981.

11. McCrady, Ellen.   "National Preservation Program Con-
    ference," The Abbey Newsletter 5(6):67-70, 1981.

12. _____ .   "Priorities in Library and Archival Con-
    servation," The Abbey Newsletter 5(2):17-19, 1981.

13. Darling, Pamela. "Preservation: Today on a Shoe-string, Tomorrow...?" Library Journal, 105:781-85, April 1, 1980.

14. See "National Conservation Advisory Council," American Institute for Conservation Newsletter 5(4):6-7, 1980.

15. Discussion Paper on a National Institute for Conservation of Cultural Property. Washington: National Conservation Advisory Council, 1978.

16. Proposal For A National Institute For The Conservation Of Cultural Property. Washington: National Conservation Advisory Council, 1982.

17. Report of the Study Committee on Libraries and Archives. Washington: National Conservation Advisory Council, 1978.

18. Report from the Regional Centers Study Committee to the National Conservation Advisory Council. Washington: NCAC 1976.

19. Brahm, Walter. An Appraisal of the Need for Conservation Facilities and Services by Ohio Libraries. Cleveland: Case Western Reserve University, 1978.

20. Russell, J. R. (ed.). Preservation of Library Materials. New York: Special Libraries Assn, 1980.

21. Final Narrative Report of the Institute on the Development and Administration of Programs for the Preservation of Library Materials. 1978. Washington: National Endowment for the Humanities, 1978.

22. Breuer, J. Michael. Toward a California Document Conservation Program. San Jose: California Library Authority for Systems and Services, 1979.

23. Brock, Jo Ann. A Program for the Conservation and Preservation of Library Materials in the General Library. Berkeley: University of California, 1975.

24. See Oklahoma Librarian 30(4): October 1979 for the complete proceedings of this gathering.

25.   Final Report--Western States Materials Conservation
      Project.   Denver: Western Council of State Li-
      braries, 1980.

26.   Report of the Task Group on the Preservation of Li-
      brary Materials.   Davis, California: The Univer-
      sity Library, 1977.

27.   "New York Conference on Book Papers and Book Pres-
      ervation," Library of Congress Information Bulletin
      38(31):298-300, 1979.

28.   The Committee on Production Guidelines for Book
      Longevity: Interim Report on Book Paper, April
      1981.   Washington: The Council on Library Re-
      sources, 1981.

Chapter III

MAJOR CONSERVATION PROGRAMS TODAY

The number and scope of the programs in all aspects of
conservation today are such that it is difficult to accept that
not too many years ago most librarians and archivists had
the philosophical conviction that the preservation of books
and records was of secondary importance when compared to
the collection, organization, arrangement, and description of
their collections. The consensus of a group of distinguished
librarians interrogated by Dudley Weiss in the fifties was
that "Librarians are service oriented; few know very much
about the physical book, and fewer still are interested in
learning or doing anything about it."[1] Only a few years before Weiss's wide-scale enquiry, Pelham Barr was shoveling
sand against the tide when he wrote "Silence, rarely broken,
seems to surround the subject of book conservation....
Conservation is the only library function which should be
continuously at work twenty-four hours a day."[2]

How different is the situation now when most of the
important conservation programs have been conceived by and
are being managed by librarians and archivists. With the
wholehearted support of conservators, curatorial and administrative staffs are now working singly in their own establishments or collectively with others (in the face of what are
sometimes prohibitive costs for replacement, reproduction,
or restoration) to keep their collections usable for today's
patrons and preserve them for those in the future.

In this chapter we bring to your attention a variety
of programs that illustrate the now wholesome outlook for
conservation, and that librarians and archivists have, in
general, accepted this important function as their responsibility and have decided to take charge. As in Chapter II,
this is only a cross section of what is going on with projects
selected because they illustrate what can be accomplished

with different levels of effort.   Failure to mention any program underway or already completed is not a suggestion that
it is of less significance than those described herein.   In
keeping with the plan of this book, we have included only
North American programs.   The Bollettino dell'Istituto Centrale per la Patologia del Libro [4857], Studies in Conservation [4777], Paper Conservation News [10836] and other journals listed in the bibliography, Chapter IX, faithfully report
progress elsewhere.   Each issue of the ALA Yearbook records programs in progress for that year under the "Preservation of Library Materials" heading.

The LBI Book Testing Laboratory

The three programs for the mass deacidification of books,
two still being perfected in 1982 and one now available for
use, will be described in Chapter V.   Another technical
program of particular interest to us is the Library Binding
Institute's Book Testing Laboratory at the Rochester Institute
of Technology. [3]   Its purpose is to educate graphic arts students on the technology and importance of library binding,
building strength into volumes for library use, and participating in research and development of materials and equipment.   Professor Rebsamen, chief of the laboratory, con-
ducts seminars and workshops for publishing and book production executives, and technical supervisors, as well as
those who are responsible for the care of books.

The Center for the Book

Public Law 95-129 signed by President Carter on October 13,
1977 established the Center for the Book in the Library of
Congress to serve as a focal point for those concerned with
the current conditions and future prospects for books and
other paper-based materials.   Amongst its wide interest is
preservation of the book.   It is hoped that this national program will be an effective catalyst for programs in connection
with the physical care of materials in libraries and archives.
Perhaps, too, the Center might be able to resolve some of
the subtle conflicts between the functionaries of some professional affiliations, both public and private, whose dedication
to "the cause" is unquestioned, but whose positions on some
issues sometimes appear to be self-serving.

The National Institute for the Conservation of Cultural Property, Inc.

Underlying the design of the National Institute, the successor in April 1982 to the National Conservation Advisory Council, Inc. (see Chapter II, page 18) is the intent to further develop and implement a national policy for preserving the cultural heritage of the United States. The Institute's objectives are to build public understanding of conservation principles and problems and to achieve new levels of sustained funding for preservation from both public and private sources. Initially many of its activities will be directed toward developing public support through educational programs. Support services for existing preservation efforts and for those responsible for conservation will grow on a parallel course. The membership of the Institute, which is incorporated as a nonprofit organization in the District of Columbia in order to have financial independence, is composed of representatives of government and private institutions representing all aspects of conservation. The new institute will undoubtedly support the NCAC's studies on library and archives conservation[4] and regional centers[5] and pursue the NCAC's recommendations for a nationwide information, education, and scientific support service. [6]

American Institute for Conservation

The American Institute for Conservation (AIC), formerly the American Group-International Institute for Conservation, now headquartered in Washington, is a private nonprofit corporation "formed to provide an organization for persons engaged in the conservation and restoration of historic and artistic works in order that they may exchange, coordinate and advance knowledge and improve methods of art conservation and restoration."[7] Its initial objective to become nationally effective as an agency for continuing education and the advancement of knowledge in the conservation field has been realized. The goals of the AIC and its affiliated Foundation of the American Institute for Conservation (FAIC), a fund-raising establishment, are essentially the same as those of the NCAC--including somewhat cautious support for a national institute for conservation. [8] The first official business meeting of the Book and Paper Group--AIC was in May 1981. The presence of 175 conferees at that meeting is evidence of the ever-increasing interest by professional conservators in book and document repair and res-

toration. The Book and Paper Group will be an influence
in policy formulations in the AIC and in national and regional efforts. The Smithsonian Institution's Preservation
Analytical Laboratory has long had a leading role in the development of preservation techniques, including paper objects. The Smithsonian's Institute of Museum Services'
staff as well as the laboratory staff are sympathetic with
and participate actively in the activities of the AIC. This,
however, has not prevented some concern on the part of
some members of the AIC in regard to the Smithsonian's
proposals for the establishment of a conservation training
program on a national scale in Washington. [9]

National Preservation Office

There is now a National Preservation Office in the Library
of Congress with a National Preservation Officer to coordinate efforts on the part of the Library of Congress to provide direct and indirect service to the library, archive, and
preservation communities in accordance with the consensus
of the participants at the planning conference in Washington
in December 1976. [10] The overwhelming size and complexity
of preservation problems facing librarians are a momentous
challenge to this office in the Library of Congress which,
logically, should be the establishment on the national level
to organize and administer a nationwide library conservation
program for all libraries. Similarly, the National Archives
and Records Services (NARS), if it had not closed down its
preservation research laboratory (for the second time in
twenty years) in February 1982, could have been the establishment at the national level providing leadership and guidance for all local, state, and regional efforts in archives
and records conservation programs.

In 1982 NARS preservation microfilm conservation
efforts are directed inward with emphasis on the development of an inspection plan for archives microfilm, the study
of the deterioration of magnetic tape and microfilm, and the
design of a statistical survey procedure to evaluate their paper holdings for preservation purposes.

Society of American Archivists

The Society of American Archivists provides conservation
leadership on a national level for archives and records cen-

ters through the activities of its Conservation Professional
Affinity Group's committees and its publications: The American Archivist, The Basic Manual Series, and monographs
on a wide variety of subjects.   Its basic archival conservation program in 1982, National Endowment for the Humanities funded, included twelve two-day preservation workshops
at various locations throughout the country and an ongoing
conservation consultant service.   These conservation consultants assist archival institutions in evaluating environmental conditions, collections maintenance, security systems,
exhibition practices, and archival procedures from a conservation perspective.

American Library Association

The long concern of the American Library Association with
the problem of the care of books need not be extolled here.
The early primary interest of the Committee on Preservation of Library Materials on bookbinding expanded rapidly
in the latter part of the 1970s into interest in permanent/
durable paper and a broad range of other subjects related
to book care with ever-increasing participation during the
annual meetings in the discussion groups and workshops related to book conservation.

In 1979 preservation reached full equality with other
ALA activities when the association's Preservation Committee was expanded into a Preservation of Library Materials
Section within the Resources and Technical Services Division
with an original membership of 1300 librarians.   This dy-
namic group will have much influence in matters relating to
all forms of bookbinding and repair, education, quality of
library materials, and other aspects of library conservation
as study committees are formed within the new section.
Further evidence of the growing attention to conservation in
other divisions of the ALA was the "Technical Service Directors of Large Libraries Discussion Group" at the 1981
ALA meeting in San Francisco in which the participants,
among other things, talked about preservation. [11]

A particularly interesting conservation-related effort
is the work of Ad Hoc Committee on Security of the Rare
Books and Manuscripts Section, Association of College and
Research Libraries. [12]   Responding to the rash of thefts in
1979 and 1980, it is compiling information on the subject to
identify and center security responsibilities in an institution

and create greater awareness on the part of legal and law
enforcement authorities. The committee is examining the
need for aids such as manuals, guidelines, cooperative theft
announcements, and recovery mechanisms, and will strength-
en its ties with the antiquarian book trade and the Society
of American Archivists.

Kentucky Conservation Program

The State Librarian and Commissioner for Libraries and
Archives in Kentucky has created a Conservation Advisory
Committee for the Department for Libraries and Archives
and charged its members to investigate the situation in the
Commonwealth and recommend short- and long-range programs for the preservation of records of Kentucky's heritage
in all records keeping establishments in the State.   This
program has the support of the Kentucky Library Association, the Kentucky Council on Archives, the Kentucky Historical Society, and other professional groups.

Western Conservation Congress

At the colloquium in Snowbird, Utah terminating the Western
States Materials Conservation Project (see page 20), the
participants ensured the continued impact of decisions made
during the meeting by voting to form the Western Conservation Congress. [13] Members of the Congress, having drawn
up a constitution and bylaws, stipulated a three-phase plan
for conservation.   First, the establishment of a clearinghouse that would also be a focus for library and archives
conservation in the Western United States.   Second, the creation of services to supplement clearinghouse action, such
as a microfilm repository, an insurance pool, and cooperative purchases of supplies and equipment.   The third phase,
and long-range objective, is the establishment of a network
of laboratories in the West.   To their everlasting credit,
Western Council of States Libraries' members from Oregon,
Arizona, Nebraska, Nevada, Wyoming, Alaska, Colorado,
Iowa, and Oklahoma have pledged to support and strengthen
new Western Conservation Congress Chapters in their states.

Conservation activities in fourteen other Western
states are attributable to the initial efforts in those states
by the Western States Materials Conservation Project.   Illustrative of those is the Colorado Conservation Study done

by the Northeast Document Conservation Center and paid for
with LSCA Title III funds and administered by the Colorado
State Library.   The program included surveys of fifteen libraries and archives with written evaluations of their buildings and environments as they relate to conservation needs
of the collections, and assessments of the storage, handling,
and conditions of the collections.   Phase III of the program
was a conservation seminar series in Colorado for all libraries and archives.   The major outcome of the project
was a written plan for library materials conservation in
Colorado, part of which is a needs assessment manual. [14]
This manual derives directly from the work and conservation survey methodology developed at the New England Document Conservation Center from 1973 to 1978.   The step-by-
step question and answer technique, using prepared forms
for recording data, is applicable to any library or archive
regardless of size.

Coordinated conservation activities in the Western
United States began at the Snowbird Conference in 1980.   It
is difficult to understand why requests for funding these
well-conceived, follow-up projects which will benefit hundreds of libraries and archives in many states have been
rejected by the national funding agencies, which, not too
long ago, made very large sums of money available to single
institutions in the East for conservation use.

The Association of Research Libraries Program

In 1980 Pamela Darling began work as a preservation specialist for the Association of Research Libraries to manage
the ARL's Special Preservation Project. [15]   She and her co-
workers will design and test a self-study procedure to enable
academic librarians to identify and address preservation
problems.   The three major phases of the project are: 1)
to assemble existing materials and the expertise of those
who are knowledgeable in library conservation and draft a
set of conservation manuals on environment control, handling
and shelving, binding, mending and repair, restoration, replacement, and reproduction; 2) to test the materials, including proposals for a structural approach to conservation
management, in three different library settings; 3) to evaluate the effectiveness of the proposed planning procedures and
manuals and when satisfied, publish the finished results.
This program will have a widespread effect on conservation
management practices.

The Illinois Cooperative Conservation Program

The Illinois Cooperative Conservation Program 1981-1982,
directed by Carolyn Clarke Morrow, Morris Library, Southern Illinois University, makes use of other existing programs in the State Library system to provide basic guidance
and information to over 1200 libraries. Although the managers of the program and the Advisory Board foresee a regional treatment center sometime in the future, such was
not included in the original schedule. Emphasis was, in-
stead, on the establishment of an information center, workshops at Carbondale and in the field, a newsletter, distribution of training materials, and disaster control. This
cooperative conservation program could be used as a model
for similar programs on a state or regional basis anywhere. [16]

New York Botanical Garden Book Preservation Center

Typical of a local library preservation program in a metropolitan area is the Book Preservation Center established at
the New York Botanical Garden in 1979. [17] The staff there
serve as a clearinghouse for conservation information for
libraries in New York City, particularly those in the Bor-
ough of the Bronx. It provides basic guidance, training
programs, and instruction in simple repairs that can and
should be undertaken in-house. The staff spends much time
on the premises of participating libraries helping evaluate
climate and storage conditions, conditions of the collections,
and suggesting preventive conservation measures to reduce
damage. This is an outstanding example of how inspired
leadership in an area can result in uniformly effective, sensible in-house conservation programs and get maximum return on the investment of seed money provided for conservation by public and private sources.

Other Conservation Programs

The coordination of programs for the preservation of the
collections in consortiums of libraries within a single university are facilitated when very large sums of public and/or
private funds are made available for that purpose. Examples are the programs at Harvard[18] and Yale. [19] Although
these major university library programs are not considered
to be examples generally applicable to the many thousands
of other libraries in the country with smaller, but equally

dilapidated collections, the "trickle down" effect is useful and important.

The Stanford University conservation program[20] with emphasis on prevention by good management, including eliciting the cooperation of staff and users and realistic methods for the indoctrination of staff, faculty, and students, is excellent guidance for librarians in any library of any size. A somewhat different, but another extremely good proposal for a general conservation program, is that by Jo Ann Brock[21] for the University of California, Berkeley. This is one of several equally good study papers and program outlines developed in the University of California statewide library system.

Greater Cincinnati/Dayton, Miami Valley Library Consortium

Informal gatherings of Cincinnati librarians beginning in 1973 for the purpose of discussing mutual management problems have developed into a metropolitan library cooperative with thirty academic, public, school, and special library members from five counties. [22] Amongst this important regional library consortium's goals are affordable, local, continuing education efforts in a wide range of library management areas including conservation. Its series of institutes and workshops dealing with conservation has included sessions on binding, basic book repair, disaster preparedness, and recovery from disaster. These continuing education opportunities will continue indefinitely. One excellent result of the disaster preparedness workshop was the creation of a joint disaster preparedness task force with the neighboring Dayton/Miami Valley Consortium of libraries from the southern Ohio/northern Kentucky area.

In all of the programs for the care, repair, and restoration of library and archival materials mentioned in the preceding pages and many other fine programs in existence or being developed, there is general agreement on overall goals. Those are in essence the six conservation objectives at the Indiana State Library:

> Preventive care
> Repair and restoration
> Tests and evaluation
> Long- and short-range plans
> Cooperative programs
> Education and training

They should be yours.

References

1. Weiss, Dudley A. "Upon Looking Back," The Library
   Scene 10(3):24-28, 1981.

2. Barr, Pelham. "Book Conservation and University Library Administration," College and Research Libraries 7:214, 219, July 1946.

3. Rebsamen, Werner. "LBI Booktesting Laboratory At-
   tracts Publishers and Book Manufacturers," Library
   Scene 7(2):21-22, 1978.

4. Report of the Study Committee on Libraries and Archives. Washington: National Conservation Advisory
   Council, 1978.

5. Report from the Regional Center Study Committee.
   Washington: National Conservation Advisory Council, 1976.

6. "National Conservation Advisory Council" in American
   Institute for Conservation Preprints. (pp. 48-52)
   Washington: American Institute for Conservation,
   1980.

7. Articles of Incorporation of the American Institute for
   Conservation of Historic and Artistic Works, Inc.

8. See Minutes of the 9th Annual Business Meeting AIC,
   May 29, 1981 (attachment #5).

9. American Institute for Conservation Newsletter 5(2):1-2,
   1980.

10. A National Preservation Program: Proceedings of the
    Planning Conference. Washington: Library of Con-
    gress, 1980.

11. See American Library Association, Resources and Tech-
    nical Services Division Newsletter. Sept./Oct. 1981.

12. Library of Congress Information Bulletin 39(33):295,
    August 15, 1980.

13. Lowell, Howard P. Final Report: Western States
    Materials Conservation Project. 1980. Available

from William Knott, WCC Secretary-Treasurer, 10200 West 20th Ave., Lakewood, Colorado 80215.

14. Lowell, Howard (ed.). Planning for Conservation: A Needs Assessment Manual. Denver: Colorado State Library, 1981.

15. The Research Libraries Group News. Issue No. 11, July 1980 and in "Finally a Preservation Project Par Excellence," Library Scene 10(1):6, 1981.

16. For more information contact ICCP Project Director, Morris Library, Southern Illinois University, Carbondale, Illinois 62901.

17. Reed, Judith. "A Nucleus of Guidance, A Center for Preservation," Library Scene 9(3):12-13, 1980.

18. "Preservation at Harvard," Conservation Administration News No. 6, February, 1981.

19. "Preservation at Yale," Conservation Administration News No. 1, June 1979.

20. For information contact The Conservation Officer, Conservation Office, The Stanford University Libraries, Stanford, California 94305.

21. Brock, Jo Ann. A Program for the Conservation and Preservation of Library Materials in the General Library. Berkeley: University of California, 1975.

22. Albrecht, Cheryl. "A Library Consortium's Special Interest in Conservation," Library Scene 10(4):20-21, 1981.

Chapter IV

EDUCATION AND TRAINING

In 1973 it was Richard Buck's hope that university level
courses in conservation administration would be made available for the nonscientist and nonconservator.[1] Paul Banks,
long a leading advocate for formal training for library conservators and conservation technicians,[2] as early as 1977
wrote of the necessity for training in conservation as a specialty in a library school which has a strong commitment to
the physical book.[3]

    These wishes became a reality with the establishment
in September 1981 of the conservation and preservation programs at Columbia University's School of Library Service.[4]
The three-year graduate level Program for Conservators of
Library and Archival Materials includes two years of academic study, followed by a year's internship in an institutional conservation laboratory leading to the degree of Master
of Science in Library Service, plus a Certificate in Library
and Archives Conservation. This is a joint offering with the
Conservation Center of New York University. A second program, for Preservation Administrators, can be either a two-
year course leading to a Master of Science (Library Service)
degree and certificate for those entering without a Master's
Degree in library service or one year of study leading to a
Certificate in Library and Archives Conservation for those
entering with a Master's Degree. Paul Banks deserves
much credit for his leading role in this vital aspect of library conservation which he formally proposed in the 1979
Library Journal series on preservation.[5]

    The relatively few men and women who complete this
advanced education (six per year from the three-year program and twelve from the conservation administration program) will be far too few to meet the needs of the library
profession, but it is hoped that other colleges of library and

information science that are now offering single courses in
conservation administration will follow the lead of Columbia.
Perhaps the most profitable use of the early graduates from
Columbia would be to offer them teaching positions at other
schools of library science to replicate the Columbia program.

It is paradoxical that although there will be for a
long time to come a widespread need for training opportunities in conservation management at the continuing education
level in regional, state, and local library organizations,
many contend that this cannot be met because of the shortage
of highly trained and experienced conservators to provide this
instruction.   This point of view, however, was refuted as
early as 1975 by a committee of the National Conservation
Advisory Council[6] when the committee concluded that:

> It is possible that it will be difficult to locate trained con-
> servation personnel to teach such courses for archives
> and libraries especially for the advanced courses.   How-
> ever there is ample technical literature, a cadre of knowl-
> edgeable library and archives educators, who can master
> the available literature in the field, to sponsor such
> courses.
>
> It should be emphasized, however, that such a shortage
> of 'advanced experts' should not deter or delay the prompt
> establishment of conservation courses for practising ar-
> chivists and librarians.   The established archival and li-
> brary programs are already available.   Educators, with
> some experience in conservation and with a familiarity
> with the substantial body of conservation (literature), are
> available now.   The limited number of 'advanced' profes-
> sionals can be used as consultants in establishing courses;
> offering special lectures on a variety of technical subjects
> and training persons in advanced courses.

The opportunities nationwide for college level training
and education at a less intensive scale than at Columbia are
summarized regularly in the American Library Association's
Preservation Education Flyer. [7] Each issue of this publication lists:

I.   Preservation Education in Library Schools accredited
      by the ALA
II.   Institutions offering courses on Workshops on or in-
      cluding Preservation
III. Related Educational Opportunities
IV.   Training in Conservation
V.   Programs offered abroad

The Society of American Archivists' Education Directory: Careers and Courses in Archival Administration[8] indicates where conservation is included in the courses offered by the various colleges and universities listed. The Guild of Book Workers' frequently updated list of opportunities for training in bookbinding[9] is useful for heads of establishments who wish to upgrade the binding skills of employees in existing in-house workshops or who are considering the establishment of small workshops for case binding, binding repairs, box making, etc.

The Society of American Archivists for several years has been offering independent study courses of short duration at various locations throughout the country in the care and repair of records.[10] Training opportunities in conservation management at the continuing education level are regularly offered by regional, state, and local library organizations in New England, New York, and New Jersey sponsored by the State library associations, funded to a great extent by federal agencies and conducted by the Northeast Document Conservation Center.[11] There is no reason why conservation seminars and workshops cannot be made available anywhere in the United States with local sponsorship. One example of how this is being extremely well done in southern Ohio is briefly described in The Library Scene.[12] The NEDCC[11] is always available for consultation in these matters.

There are many opportunities for training in the preservation and restoration of photographic materials at the Rochester Institute of Technology, including long-term programs at the academic level and frequent short courses to meet special requirements. The College of Graphic Arts and Photography at RIT should be regarded as the prime source for up-to-date reliable information on all aspects of the preservation and restoration of photographic images, including teaching and training. Librarians and archivists with such materials in their collections, in order to keep fully informed on technical developments, education opportunities, and the published literature, should subscribe to PhotographiConservation,[13] the journal published regularly by RIT's Technical and Education Center of the Graphic Arts.

To summarize, more and more opportunities for formal training and education in library conservation are becoming available. There are also frequent opportunities for participation in local seminars and workshops throughout the country. Finally, the published literature is voluminous and comprehensive so that when one has not had formal training or participated in informal sessions on special aspects of book care that person can, as suggested by Paul Banks in 1978[2] read, become affiliated with professional conservation associations and conservation oriented groups (or at least subscribe to their publications), study bookbinding and related subjects, and otherwise attempt to keep in touch with the field.

Formal training and education in conservation management is highly desirable as is frequent participation in local seminars and workshops, but lack of those opportunities is no reason to despair or neglect the care of collections.

References

1.   Buck, Richard.   "On Conservation," Museum News 52(1):15-16, 1973.

2.   Banks, Paul.   "Professional Training in Library and Archives Conservation," Abbey Newsletter 3(1):1-2, 1979.

3.   _____. "Preservation of Library Materials," Encyclopedia of Library and Information Science, Vol. 23. New York: Marcel Dekker, 1977.

4.   Conservation and Preservation Programs, School of Library Service, Columbia University, New York, N. Y. 10027.

5.   Banks, Paul.   "Education for Conservation," Library Journal 104:1013-17, May 1, 1979.

6.   Report on Education and Training for Conservation in Libraries and Archives.   Prepared by the Sub-committee on Libraries and Archives of the Education and Training Committee, National Conservation Advisory Council, August 1975.

7.   Swartzburg, Susan and Susan B. White (eds.).   Preservation Education Flyer.   Chicago: American Library Association, Resources and Technical Services Division (annually).

8. Careers and Courses in Archival Administration. Chi-
    cago: Society of American Archivists, 1981.

9. Opportunities for Study in Hand Bookbinding and Related
    Crafts. New York: Guild of Book Workers, 1981.

10. For more information on the SAA's training and educa-
    tion programs write to the Society of American Ar-
    chivists, 330 S. Wells St. (Suite 810), Chicago,
    Illinois 60606.

11. For more information contact The Field Service Direc-
    tor, Abbot Hall, School Street, Andover, Massachu-
    setts 01810.

12. Albrecht, Cheryl. "A Library Consortium's Special
    Interest in Conservation," Library Scene 10(4):20-
    21, 1981.

13. PhotographiConservation: a forum of photographic pres-
    ervation and restoration. Rochester, New York:
    Technical and Education Center of the Graphic Arts,
    Rochester Institute of Technology. Vol. 1, No. 1,
    1979+.

Chapter V

PROFESSIONAL CONSERVATION

"Professional conservation is the combined efforts of scientists and conservators relating to the maintenance of the aesthetic, structural or functional integrity of objects or structures."[1] Conservators are concerned with preservation, i. e. maintenance to protect objects from harm, damage, or danger and restoration, which is renewal from a defective or incomplete state after methodical examination of materials to identify impairment and the causes of the same. The scientist "provides the conservator with the technical advice and guidance in the recognition and behavior of materials.... Although the scientist has become an essential member of the conservation team, he is not usually referred to as a conservator unless his activities extend to the treatment of objects."[2] The concept of professional conservation, according to the charter of the International Institute for Conservation of Historic and Artistic Works, includes measures "to protect and preserve and to maintain the condition and the integrity of any object or structures which because of their history, significance, rarity or workmanship have common accepted value and importance for the common good." It includes studies "necessary to determine the nature or properties of materials used in any kinds of cultural holdings, or in their housing, handling or treatment." It further entails studies "to further the understanding and controlling of the causes of deterioration of historic and artistic works."[3] Conservators and scientists are the other two categories of specialists in the tripartite concept of conservation (see Figure 2) from whom librarians and archivists get guidance and counsel for preventive conservation programs and basic in-house treatment of books and documents. The conservators are the highly trained and experienced specialists to whom librarians should send the twenty percent of their damaged materials requiring sophisticated treatment that should never be attempted in-house, unless there is a con-

servator or qualified conservation technician on the staff
(see Chapter VIII).

Scientists and paper conservators whose services are
available to custodians are listed in the directory of the
American Institute for Conservation. [4]   Book restorers,
highly specialized conservators, are listed in the AIC directory and the directory of the Guild of Book Workers. [5]   The
preservation of Library Materials Section, Resources and
Technical Services Division, American Library Association[6a]
will provide names of specialists in preventive and restorative conservation of library materials.   Similarly, the Society of American Archivists[6b] will supply names of specialists who can provide reliable information on archives and
records conservation programs.

The conservation scientist's domain is the laboratory
where he is continually investigating the chemical and physical characteristics of materials and the effect of their sur-
roundings on them.   An example is the continuing research
by chemists in paper mill laboratories to further the development of permanent/durable alkaline book papers to
eliminate the "brittle book" problem.   This was begun by
Edwin Sutermeister at an S. D. Warren Paper Company mill
in Maine in the early 19th century and has continued in the
industry ever since.   Of much interest to librarians is the
early work done by W. J. Barrow which was continued at the
W. J. Barrow Research Laboratory until 1977. [7]   Excellent
reports on the scope of present day research in paper chemistry are available in the American Chemical Society's Advances in Chemical Series, Numbers 164[8] and 193. [9]

The Institute of Book Pathology founded by Alfonso
Gallo in Rome in the 1930s has been continually engaged in
the investigation of the chemistry of paper since then.   This
research is faithfully reported in that establishment's bul-
letins. [10]   The concern of scientists at the Institute of Paper
Chemistry in Appleton, Wisconsin is chemistry related to
the production of paper in all its forms for industry.   However, many of their numerous publications, particularly their
series of bibliographies on various aspects of paper chemistry, are of importance to conservators and conservation administrators. [11, 12]

Frequent reinvestigation of materials and processes
is characteristic of laboratory people to satisfy themselves
that results of former studies are sound, or when field ap-

plication of laboratory research uncovers new problems. A
typical example is the doubt lately raised by Catherine Sease
in regard to the use of soluble nylon, long a mainstay in
museum and library conservation. [13]   Conservators and conservation administrators try to keep abreast of scientific research and the developments in paper chemistry and other
conservation-related laboratory studies.

Mass Treatments

The conservator, who is in closer contact with the "owners"
of collections, works with scientists to convert the results
of laboratory studies into useful applications for preservation.   The emphasis now is to study and devise methods for
mass treatment of materials rather than single objects.
Mass treatment of library and archival materials has been
extensively developed in connection with disaster recovery.
This was begun by the recovery teams at Florence who ex-
perimented with tobacco drying sheds, industrial ovens, and
industrial vacuum fumigators for the treatment of the hundreds
of thousands of wet books they had to salvage [4278].

Freeze Stabilization

Since Florence and the later fire and flood disasters at Tem-
ple University Law Library, the St. Louis Records Center,
the Stanford University Library, and others there has been
a considerable amount of study on methods for drying great
quantities of wet books.   These investigations were reviewed
in a paper presented at the paper symposium during the 1976
American Chemical Society Meeting in San Francisco. [14]
Vacuum drying, solvent extraction, and the use of micro-
wave and dielectric energy all have been tried with some
success; but today the generally accepted method for the
mass treatment of great numbers of books after freeze
stabilization on the scene is freeze drying in industrial
vacuum chambers or with laboratory equipment.

Climate control, including control of natural and artificial light, good housekeeping and storage practices are in
effect mass treatments for materials; but they are usually
categorized as preventive conservation (see Chapter VI).
Vacuum fumigation with ethylene oxide[15] to destroy insect
and fungus infestations and freeze stabilization and freeze
drying were the dramatic developments in the mass treatment
of library and archival materials in the 1970s.

Mass Deacidification

A method for deacidification of quantities of books in a vacuum chamber using morphaline gas was developed at the
W. J. Barrow Research Laboratory before its demise. [17]
This system which is marketed by Research Corporation,
New York City[18] will neutralize mildly acid books, but it
does not introduce a buffering agent into the paper to inhibit
reacidification.

The Public Archives of Canada working with Richard
Smith has further developed Smith's highly successful method for the nonaqueous deacidification of single books into a
system for mass deacidification with magnesium methyl carbonate. [19] This system can handle up to forty books in a
single four hour cycle for a total of about 240 deacidified
and buffered books in a twenty-four hour period. This nonaqueous liquid chemical process will deacidify and buffer
even extremely acid book pages with little or no effects on
most covers and bindings. When this system is made available for general use it will be a boon for libraries and archives.

Scientists at the Library of Congress working first
with engineers at the General Electric Space Center in Valley Forge and now at the Goddard Space Center in Green-
belt, Maryland are perfecting a method for mass deacidification and buffering several thousand books at a time in a
vacuum chamber using diethyl zinc as the agent. [20] The
completion of these studies is also anxiously awaited by conservators and conservation administrators because of the
number of volumes that can be treated at one time.

Mass deacidification, a great step forward in the conservation of library materials, is bound to have a profound
effect on conservation programs. It is only by mass deacidification of books that the library profession can ever
hope to keep usable in codex form the tens and even hundreds of thousand of books in single establishments and the
hundreds of millions of books in libraries throughout the
country that will otherwise crumble to dust. Mass deacidification is not a panacea. [16] It is, however, another tool
available to librarians which will enable them to help keep
usable books in which the information they contain cannot or
should not be transferred to another form for preservation.

The already available morpholine process and the
forthcoming diethyl zinc and magnesium methylcarbonate

systems will all require a large capital investment. It would
seem logical to have these systems located in various parts
of the country in: a) regional conservation centers; b) state
libraries or archives; or c) owned by library consortiums,
for their own uses and for use by others for a fee. The
American Library Association, and local, state, and regional
library affiliations throughout the country should carefully
evaluate the alternative mass deacidification systems now
and plan for the maximum utilization of one or another as
soon as possible. This is a major challenge to those professional groups.

Additional Regional Centers for Professional Services

In 1974 Richard Buck described a regional conservation center as "an agency which can provide services in conservation to a certain geographical area."[21] He then related
how (as we have outlined in Chapter I of this book) membership in a regional center would be beneficial. What Buck
predicted has become a fact with the establishment of several very successful regional conservation centers for museums. The single center primarily for libraries, archives
and public record centers, The Northeast Document Conservation Center (NEDCC) established in 1973 as a nonprofit
establishment, has also prospered.

The NEDCC is a model for other regional conservation efforts for the benefit of libraries and archives, but no
group elsewhere has attempted to provide the full range of
services available to libraries and archives in the Northeast
from the NEDCC. At first glance this seems illogical, but
on close examination the reasons are plausible. Ann Russell, Director NEDCC, analyzed this matter in a paper presented to a panel on cooperation in conservation at the 1980
Society of American Archivists meeting in Cincinnati. No
one could have done it better. With Russell's permission
we have abridged that extremely important presentation for
the users of this book. For the complete text see the Win-
ter 1982 American Archivist.[22]

> NEDCC presently serves 300 non-profit institu-
> tions per year through its laboratory and consulting
> services. It reaches at least 1,000 more each
> year through its educational programs. Further,
> the Center is now more or less self-supporting
> through fees for its services. It has an annual

operating budget in excess of $500,000 and em-
ploys a staff of 20-22.   The unspoken question in
my mind, and I'm sure in many others is why no
other region has followed New England's example.

NEDCC was founded in 1973 by the New England
Library Board.   Start-up funds were provided by
the New England Library Board and the Council on
Library Resources, as well as other contributors.
Prime movers in drafting and implementing the
original prospectus were Rockwell Potter, Administrator of Public Records for Connecticut; Walter
Brahm, then State Librarian of Connecticut; and
George Cunha, conservator of the Boston Athenaeum, who was to become the NEDCC's first Director.

The Center was created to be a shared facility,
making available the expertise for restoring documents and books to all non-profit institutions in the
region.   The Center's founders recognized that because of the high cost of setting up and staffing an
in-house conservation laboratory most libraries
and archives would never have their own conservation facilities.   It seemed that conservation was a
problem that could be most effectively addressed
on a cooperative basis, as opposed to an institu-
tion-by-institution approach.   Today, the Center's
laboratory services are virtually self-supporting,
but the Center's education programs and free disaster assistance service are not cost-recovering,
nor are they factored into the charge for laboratory
services.   For these activities, the Center is reli-
ant on outside grant support.

For seven years NEDCC was legally an arm of
the New England Library Board.   In September,
1980, the Center incorporated as a non-profit corporation, changing its name from New England
Document Conservation Center to Northeast Document Conservation Center to reflect the expansion
of the Center's region to include New York and
New Jersey.   NEDCC is governed by a Board of
Directors, made up of Directors of state library
agencies in the eight states it serves.   NEDCC's
structure, based on membership by a state agency
which serves as an umbrella for the state, differs

from a consortium which works primarily for a group of member institutions. An advantage of NEDCC's structure is that it opens a potential market of literally thousands of institutions who may use the Center's services.

NEDCC has a large paper conservation laboratory, specializing in conservation of library and archival materials; the only one in any center which specializes in treating books, maps, and documents typical of the collections of libraries and archival institutions.

The Center has a hand bookbindery headed by an Associate Conservator. NEDCC's trademark is the "full treatment" of books. There are few facilities in the entire country that can perform this service, as most hand binders do not have training in paper conservation that enables them to salvage badly deteriorated book pages. The Center specializes in a conservation approach to binding.

The Center's newest service is its microreproduction department. It includes a preservation microfilm program and a photographic copying service. Initiated in 1978 with a grant from the National Historical Publications and Records Commission, it specializes in filming of hard-to-film materials. The microfilm service also offers assistance in preparing materials for microfilming. This department has developed a service for converting nitrate photographic negatives to safety film and producing prints from historic negatives.

The Center has a free disaster assistance service for the region it serves. This includes free consultation to any non-profit organization that has experienced a serious fire, flood or other disaster. If necessary, NEDCC will send a staff member to the scene to help assess damage and organize recovery operation. On the average, the Center receives about one disaster call per week, ranging from major floods to coping with the after effects of an intruding skunk.

The Center offers a range of educational services including onsite consultation and workshops to

help archives, libraries, and other repositories
develop better conservation programs. NEDCC's
field service work is an example of the kind of
service which only a non-profit, cooperative center
can offer.

From the start, the Center has recognized that
an important part of its function is to make available expertise and to serve as a clearinghouse for
information. One of the Center's most important
contributions, over the years, has been raising
consciousness of conservations problems among
archivists, librarians and historical society personnel.

High quality conservation treatment tends to be
expensive, even in a non-profit, partially subsidized
setting like NEDCC's. This is because the work
is highly labor intensive. It has been no easy
matter for the Center to strike a balance in pric-
ing its services. Building an active clientele is a
long process, but today the Center is sufficiently
well known and well regarded to attract an adequate volume of work. Furthermore, the extension
of the Center's region to include New York and
New Jersey has helped to increase the Center's
visibility and expand the number of potential users
of the Center's services.

Can NEDCC offer any analysis that will be valuable to other regions that seek to establish conservation facilities? Obviously an initial need is
start-up funds. More than $100,000 was needed
to equip and launch NEDCC. At today's prices,
probably two to three times this amount would be
needed. Whatever agency or agencies provide
start-up funding for a center should be prepared
to provide support for a long time, conceivably as
long as five years, before the center can be expected to become fully self-supporting. It is likely
that the educational services of a center, which
cannot be cost-recovering, will always need to be
subsidized in one way or another.

What sort of institutional base should a new center have? NEDCC's initial association with the
New England Library Board was extremely valuable

in terms of establishing credibility with potential
funding agencies. Most funding agencies prefer to
strengthen existing organizations rather than to
create a brand new organization with its own expensive superstructure and operating costs.

A fundamental concern for a new center would
be obtaining institutional commitment from potential users. If conservation services could be provided without charge, there would be almost no
limit to the demand for those services. However,
no one to date has seriously proposed to provide
a totally subsidized conservation service. Demand
for conservation services for which a fee is
charged, even a modest fee, tends to be self-
limiting. Most archives, historical organizations
and libraries do not budget for conservation on an
annual basis and are not in a position to make a
long-term commitment to a cooperative facility.

Marketing the new center's services would be
of critical importance. This is not easy when the
potential users are struggling, non-profit organizations themselves. It is difficult to offer a quality
service at prices low enough to encourage heavy
use. While start-up subsidies might make it possible to price the services below the actual cost in
the early years, a time will come eventually when
charges must reflect the real cost of doing the
work. In terms of developing a broad clientele,
NEDCC has benefitted tremendously from its location in an area of dense population. In a sparsely
populated area, it is unlikely that there would be
enough demand to support a center unless a few
major institutions would commit a large annual
budget for conservation work.

A serious problem that any new center would
confront is the shortage of professionally-trained
conservators. Most of these choose to specialize
in art on paper as opposed to library and archival
materials.

In my view, a region that wishes to replicate
NEDCC's model, or develop a model of its own,
for providing cooperative conservation services,
will find that the key ingredient is leadership.

The vision, dedication and energy of an individual
or a group of individuals will be needed to over-
come inertia and gain commitments from potential
supporters of the new venture.   The leader must
be willing to embrace what is essentially a selling
job.

Let us admit that founding and managing a cooperative conservation center is not easy to do.
The Northeast was able to get a cooperative conservation center off the ground and this fact alone
demonstrates that under certain circumstances it
can be done.   For other regions, the great challenge is stimulating investment in conservation.
This boils down to a public education effort, which,
in some sense, is the responsibility of all librarians and archivists.   All innovations tend to meet
with resistance.   Let us hope that the Northeast
example will help to convince skeptics that it is
possible to fly.

References

1.   Buck, Richard.   "On Conservation," Museum News 52(1):
        15-16, 1973.

2.   Ibid.

3.   Ibid.

4.   American Institute for Conservation, 1511 K St., N.W.,
        Suite 725, Washington, D.C. 20005.

5.   Guild of Book Workers, 663 Fifth Avenue, New York,
        New York 10022.

6.   American Library Association, 50 East Huron Street,
        Chicago, IL 60611; Society of American Archivists,
        330 S. Wells St. (Suite 810) Chicago, IL 60606.

7.   Roberson, D.D.   "Permanence/Durability and Preserva-
        tion Research at the Barrow Laboratory" in Preser-
        vation of Paper and Textiles of Historic and Artistic
        Value II.   Washington: American Chemical Society,
        1981.

Chapter VI

IN-HOUSE CONSERVATION--PREVENTION

"The responsibility of the preserving and maintain-
ing society's tremendous reserve of books rests
squarely on librarians and those associated with
librarians in all capacities."

--Dudley A. Weiss
in Library Scene, June, 1981

Pelham Barr's almost solitary concern in 1946[1] for what he
regarded as an indifferent attitude by librarians towards the
importance of binding in conservation, well-founded then, is
no longer generally applicable. Barr's nine essential points
for inclusion in the broad scope of book conservation were,
in fact, preventive conservation for books. They are: a)
selecting material before purchase with respect to usability
and useful life; b) examining condition and probable future
condition of all material received, whether by gift or purchase, and prescribing conservation treatment if necessary
before use; c) providing proper housing of all material, in
accordance with its conservation needs as well as accessibil-
ity; d) assuming responsibility for its condition at all times;
e) assuming its proper handling by staff and patrons; f) organizing systematic inspection so that the need for conservation attention is promptly recognized; g) deciding on the
proper treatment for all material needing attention; h) supervising the treatment; and i) deciding on storage or discard-
ing.

Conservation must be a continuum of actions by the
entire staff. About fifteen years ago the physical condition
of their collections had become a matter of concern to librarians and archivists, but attention to their care was not
the general practice. Even now the great majority of books
and records after having been carefully collected, organized,

and catalogued for use are deteriorating on their shelves
and in their boxes at an ever-increasing rate; even though
their custodians now have access to much information on
how to minimize deterioration and in some instances arrest
it entirely.   We have reached the point in time where widespread positive action is necessary (see Figure 1).

For some strange reason there was for a while in
the library profession the general idea that those responsible
for the books and other records, although able to handle
very efficiently the many other aspects of their work, were
not competent to oversee the physical care of those materials.   Today, emboldened by guidance and leadership from
the American Library Association and the Society of American Archivists and encouraged by some conservators, more and
more administrators and curators are accepting the fact that
by their action they can significantly extend the useful lives
of the materials that they must keep available for use.

More and more librarians now concede that it is more
sensible to invest in climate control, control of light, good
housekeeping and storage, fire protection, and protection
from theft and vandalism to minimize losses by those causes,
than to ignore preventive conservation now and pay later even
greater costs for replacement of books or for the salvage of
those that cannot be replaced.   Conservation includes: a)
prevention of damage by controlling the environments, improved storage, enhanced security; and b) basic in-house
treatment of materials already damaged.   Of the two, prevention is far more important for the obvious reason and
because money, always scarce, spent for prevention benefits
the collections as a whole (mass treatment).   This makes
prevention programs much more cost effective.   Librarians,
archivists, and other records managers also no longer accept the premise that it will not be possible to begin conservation programs in their establishments until there are a
large number of fully-trained and highly-skilled specialists
to run them.   That, of course, would be ideal--but the idea
is utopian.

Richard Buck's observations in 1973 about museum
conservation administration[2] were applicable to libraries and
archives then and still are.   He, a conservator, recognized
the emerging role of curators, directors, and others representing the "owners" of collections when he wrote that they
must:

a) have a knowledge of the condition of the objects in a collection and a surveillance of their condition
b) have an understanding of the effects of the environment on the condition of objects and a surveillance of the environment
c) (initiate) corrective action to correct defects in the condition of the objects
d) (initiate) action to correct environmental deficiencies
e) (consider) the condition of objects in scheduling exhibition and loans controlling storage and handling
f) (budget) funds to carry out any necessary action

The requirement for education and training in conservation management for administrators and curators is unquestionably equal to the need for the training of more book and paper conservators and technicians. Fortunately a good start has been made in that direction (see Chapter IV), but the requirement will exceed the availability of managers formally trained in conservation administration for some time to come. Therefore, people in policy making and management positions now must make the decisions to incorporate conservation awareness and responsibilities into the day-to-day routines of all hands and find the money to pay for it. In-house treatment of damaged materials and disaster prevention and recovery are discussed elsewhere in this book. This part is concerned with preventive conservation--those things that can be done in-house, usually with the present staff at a reasonable cost to lessen damage. Each establishment must develop and determine its own policies because the conditions in no two libraries could ever be the same, even if they had identical collections. Each and every repository must establish its own conservation programs and implement them according to the conditions that prevail there. Excellent guidance for broad policy making is in Robert Patterson's "Ten Charges to a Conservation Committee" in the Library Journal's 1979 special series on conservation. [3] An example of more specific guidance in one area of conservation implementation is Robert Schnare's views on conservation administration. [4] We can think of no better way to start than by patterning a program on their views and the excellent guidance offered by Caroline Clark Morrow[5] based on her experience at Southern Illinois University's Morris Library.

Surveys

Once organized in a modest way (or on a more ambitious
scale with a conservation advisory committee and/or a conservation coordinator), with agreement on conservation policies for your particular collection, and utilizing as many as
possible of the training opportunities (seminars, workshops,
conservation classes in continuing education programs), you
are well on the way towards some degree of control of the
situation on your premises.   Regardless of its scope and
direction, any in-house preventive conservation program
should be developed from the results of a survey.   These
inspections are designed to evaluate the building and environment as they relate to the conservation needs of the collections and to assess the storage, handling, and condition of
the various collections in the building.   When it is possible
to hire a professional conservator to do that, it should be
done.   They are skilled in detecting deleterious conditions
and applying their broad experience to the correction of the
same.   When, as is all too frequently the case, money is
not available for a professional survey, it can be done by
the staff.   The New England Document Conservation Center
from its inception encouraged librarians and others at workshops throughout the Northeast to "do it themselves" when
they could not hire NEDCC for surveys, and by 1974 was
providing librarians with printed forms to aid them.   This
encouragement and guidance was formally presented to the
library profession at a conservation seminar in Syracuse,
New York in 1976. [6]   In 1980 Howard Lowell and the Northeast Document Conservation Center staff updated and expanded the self-assessment guide[6] in connection with the
Colorado Conservation Study. [7]   Both guides describe how to
determine what are the conservation needs in a library by
answering 124 questions (using forms provided) in regard to
characteristics and the physical condition of the building;
all of the aspects of security from fire and flood to theft,
vandalism, and other disasters; and the physical condition
of those categories of materials in collections that have been
previously selected as qualifying for preventive conservation. [12]   They also include suggestions for evaluating the
collected data and for converting the conclusions made into
a written survey report, which is in essence a conservation
plan for the establishment.   A less lengthy survey guide for
archival materials compiled by the Society of American Archivists[8] can be used in conjunction with these two manuals
or by itself.

These surveys will let you know where you stand in
regard to climate control; control of light; suitability of
storage areas and facilities; the physical condition of the
books, documents, maps and atlases, broadsides, prints and
pictures, and works of art on paper for which you are responsible.   From these surveys you can determine what re-
medial measures and treatment can be done on the premises
and what should be done only by professionals.   You can
establish priorities for each and what is of utmost importance, and you can get an idea of what all this might cost
over the next ten or even twenty years.   After a survey has
given you an idea of where you stand and what must be done,
then you can start on improvements to the building, security,
environment control, and housekeeping.   For example, without resorting to new building construction or major reconstruction of existing facilities, there are ways to make
drastic improvements in climate control and control of damaging light at relatively modest costs.

Program Management

The principal causes for deterioration of materials are either
biological, physiochemical, or mechanical, acting indepen-
dently or concurrently.   See Kowalik [2345], Magida [6880],
Feller [2143] and Russell [6905].   Many have written on the
causes for decay of cultural property, but it is doubtful if
anyone has handled the broad subject in a few pages as well
as Bernard Feilden. [9]   However, it is to Plenderleith and
Werner that we are indebted for the ultimate in brevity and
completeness.   Their single-page diagram of the interrelation of the causes of decay and damage to cultural property
(see Figure 3) proves the adage that "one picture is worth
a thousand words."

Most of these enemies of materials are controllable.
Even when limitation of funds precludes the installation of
sophisticated heating, ventilation, and air conditioning systems, new lighting, sophisticated alarm systems, and so on,
a great deal can be accomplished by common sense use of
that with which one has to work.   Pamela Darling's presentation on preservation with or without money at the 1980
Oklahoma Colloquium on Conservation[10] is one of the best
of several essays on that theme.

In regard to specific aspects of preventive conservation, custodians, by selecting titles for further reading from

CAUSES OF DECAY AND DAMAGE TO CULTURAL PROPERTY*

EXTERNAL CAUSES OF DECAY: The SUN produces LIGHT with ULTRA VIOLET and HEAT RADIATION

Climatic Causes
seasonal temperature changes
daily temperature changes
precipitation of rain and snow
ice and frost
ground water and moisture in soil dust

Biological and Botanical Causes
animals
birds
insects
trees and plants
fungi, moulds, lichens

Natural Disasters
tectonics
earthquakes
tidal waves
floods
avalanches
volcanic eruptions
exceptional winds
fire

INTERNAL CAUSES OF DECAY: (Note: the building modifies and protects)

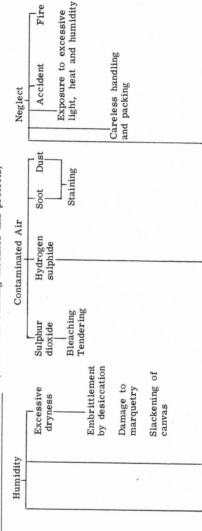

Humidity
- Excessive dryness
  - Embrittlement by desiccation
  - Damage to marquetry
  - Slackening of canvas

Contaminated Air
- Sulphur dioxide
  - Bleaching
  - Tendering
- Hydrogen sulphide
- Soot   Dust
  - Staining

Neglect
- Accident   Fire
  - Exposure to excessive light, heat and humidity
  - Careless handling and packing

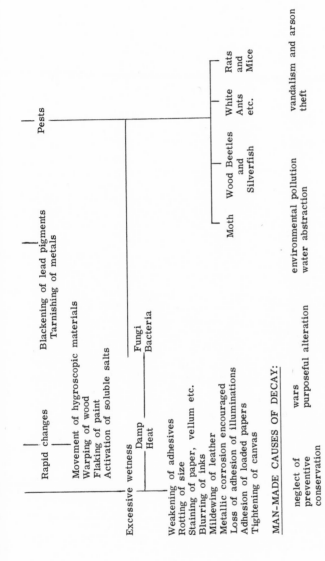

Rapid changes

Blackening of lead pigments
Tarnishing of metals

Movement of hygroscopic materials
Warping of wood
Flaking of paint
Activation of soluble salts

Excessive wetness
Damp ——— Fungi
Heat ——— Bacteria

Weakening of adhesives
Rotting of size
Staining of paper, vellum etc.
Blurring of inks
Mildewing of leather
Metallic corrosion encouraged
Loss of adhesion of illuminations
Adhesion of loaded papers
Tightening of canvas

Pests

Moth   Wood Beetles   White   Rats
            and   Ants   and
            Silverfish   etc.   Mice

MAN-MADE CAUSES OF DECAY:

neglect of   wars   environmental pollution   vandalism and arson
preventive   purposeful alteration   water abstraction   theft
conservation

*Grateful acknowledgement to H.J. Plenderleith and A.E. Werner,
The Conservation of Antiquities and Works of Art.

Figure 3.

the several hundred citations under various subheadings in
Chapter IV of the bibliography, should find more than sufficient information for their own needs.   There is such complete agreement amongst scientists, engineers, and conservators on climate control, and control of natural and artificial light as described in our Conservation of Library Materials [7261] that nothing more is necessary here.   Nor is it
necessary to dwell on housekeeping and storage, other than
to mention that those who are contemplating the use of compact shelving should obtain the report of the American Library Association's recent study of that subject. [11]   It de-
scribes a wide variety of electric, manual assist, and manual shelving systems with diagrams and photographs showing
how movable stacks can save space.   Although security seldom has ever been used as a reason for adopting compact
shelving, we suggest that in addition to the other unquestionable benefits that they are a deterrent to pilfering.   That is
because in any bank of these rolling shelves there is never
access to more than one aisle at a time and also because
of the ease of locking up the system at night.

     Selection of what in the collections should be pre-
served is preventive conservation, even though the actual
repair of those items comes under the treatment category.
Although conservators are frequently asked what in a collection should be preserved, those are management decisions
requiring consideration of many factors in addition to physical condition.   They are intellectual content, rarity, value,
importance to research, availability of the same information
in other forms, and the alternative methods for preserving
the intellectual content of worn books.   Joel Rutstein, Collection Development Librarian, Colorado State University Libraries emphasized the importance of keeping preservation
in its true perspective in relation to the other aspects of
collection development in an excellent paper presented at the
Association of College and Research Libraries 1981 conference. [12]

     Conservators can provide helpful information on the
condition of any materials and treatment required if any,
with estimated costs; but the decisions must be made by
managers.   In addition to guidance from conservators, seminars and workshops can provide learning opportunities for
the identification of various types and grades of paper; the
recognition of different kinds of book and paper deterioration;
how to estimate degrees of degradation; how to test for acid
contamination in still reasonably good looking books and docu-

ments; how to recognize the different types of bindings on
library shelves (publisher's, trade, school, hand binding,
restoration binding, etc.); and how each will stand up to the
amount of use and abuse books get from various users.
Such doctrinal sessions can also include presentations by
librarians, microform specialists, binders, and restorers
on the use of reprints and facsimilies; microforms and hard
copy from the same; commercial binding, hand binding, and
restoration binding; boxing; and even withdrawal from use of
damaged books vs. repair and restoration. All are important management decisions.

Some librarians rely on periodic stack checks by department personnel to identify volumes needing attention.
Others depend on staff and users to bring damage to their
attention. Libraries having a conservation committee and/or
a conservation administrator sometimes conduct surveys of
particular collections or categories of books to spot those
needing treatment. Sally Buchanan's and Sandra Coleman's
report of a deterioration survey in the Stanford University
Libraries, [13] which includes a detailed description of the
criteria and procedures used, could well be a guide for
a similar survey in any library. The Columbia University
Libraries' "Cul Handbook" [14] is another excellent example
of a procedure for systematic examination of books for
damage and selecting appropriate binding styles. This useful reference also contains guidelines for decision-making,
and detailed instructions on the completion of the necessary
forms. Although intended only for the Columbia University
Libraries, it is of significant interest to all university librarians.

Binding

Comprehensive binding preparation programs, good business
budget-wise, are also good preventive conservation. When
the decision is to repair worn books and the binding contractor
is required to meet rigid specifications for workmanship and
material quality, binding budgets will go farther. Librarians
have a wide range of options from inexpensive (relatively)
oversewn bindings with utilitarian machine-made covers to
sophisticated handsewn bindings in gold tooled, vegetable
tanned leather covers; and choices between. The selection
depends on the importance of a book as an object, its use,
mass and bulk, and the anticipated duration as a catalogued
item. There is still no general agreement on standards and

specifications for various categories of bookbinding, but librarians can use for guidance the Association of Research Libraries Spec Kit #35, [15] which includes (in part) seven working documents from college and university libraries on binding specifications and other planning requirements.   They should also have available for frequent reference the Library Binding Institute's recently revised "class A binding specifications" [16] for often used (non-artifact) books and the American Library Association's approved "minimum specifications for little used materials--LUMSPECS. " [17]

Book custodians, to keep themselves informed and up-to-date in book care in general and library binding (commercial) can follow the work of ALA's Preservation of Library Materials Section and subscribe to The Library Scene [10800].   A good general introduction to the fundamentals of binding for libraries is Paul Bank's essay in the Encyclopedia of Library and Information Science. [18]

As in any major undertaking a methodical approach with check lists and preprinted forms for prebinding handling (bindery preparation) of large numbers of books is recommended.   Diverse procedures have been developed in libraries throughout the country.   The New York Public Library's list of options is available in the March 1979 Library Scene. [19]   Another analysis of options for books needing attention was done by John Dean in 1978. [20]   Yale's formulation of the options is briefly described in the June, 1979 Conservation Administration News.   One of the most well coordinated university library conservation programs is that at Southern Illinois University's Morris Library.   Their system for collaboration between library department heads and conservation binding staff in selection of options for damaged books (including brittle books) is one of the best we have seen.   Although this information is not yet published, Carolyn Clark Morrow, the Conservation Librarian, will make it available upon request.   The Newberry Library, which is fortunate enough to have a photoduplication department, a bindery, and a conservation laboratory on its premises, has an ongoing "brittle book" program for volumes with friable pages that must be replaced.   An excellent description of the Newberry's procedures for identifying those books and for collaboration between bibliographer, preservation liaison, and conservator in deciding the replacement format is in the December 1981 Library Scene.

For an answer to the simple question, "When does a book have to be rebound if it is necessary to retain the

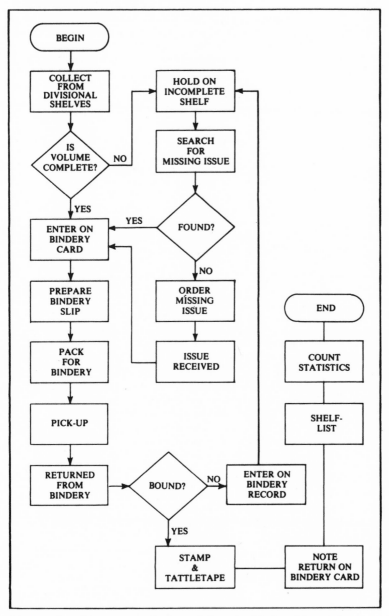

Figure 4. The maze of steps taken to bind a library's collection is simplified by this flowchart of procedures. Reprinted by permission from Library Scene, March 1981.

volume in codex form?" Martha Plowden, librarian at Clark
College in Atlanta, has devised a set of ten questions.   In
her opinion, any book for which a "yes" is applicable on
eight or more of the ten questions requires rebinding (see
page 17, September 1981 Library Scene).

        The sequence of in-house procedures and controls
that are necessary for efficient management of binding supervision and control in any library that has a large binding
budget is well illustrated by Gwen Vargas in her article on
the subject in the March 1981 Library Scene.   Her simplified flow chart of these steps is reproduced in Figure 4 by
permission of the editor of the Library Scene.

        It is needless to enlarge here on the fact that in
those libraries in which there are a significant number of
books with leather or part-leather bindings, periodic treatment with potassium lactate and a lanolin leather dressing
must be continued as a preventive conservation measure.[21]

Non-Print Materials

Because of the magnitude and complexities of the problem,
it is only possible to discuss the preservation of non-print
materials in general terms in a book such as this.   Much
has been written and much more will be written in this
decade on the subject as libraries accumulate more and
more movie and TV film, magnetic audio and video tape,
microfilm and fiche, magnetic computer tape, and later on
video and optical and sound discs.   Librarians, archivists,
and public records administrators can keep informed only by
staying up-to-date with the monographs and periodical literature.   See the bibliography (Chapter IV) which was up-to-
date in January 1982 for titles of monographs and lists of
most of the periodicals regularly published.   Brief, but con-
cise, recommendations on the care of these materials in
general by the preservation microfilming office at the Library of Congress are in the October 1980 Oklahoma Librarian.   Amongst other sources of information one should
pay particular attention to literature from the National Microfilm Association, the International Council on Archives
Microfilm Committee, The National Archives, the Library
of Congress and the U. S. Government Printing Office for
information on preservation of material on tape.

Photographic Materials

Photographic materials in a library ranging from microforms to works of art probably benefit more from preventive
conservation programs than most of the other materials in
a collection. This is because the nature of the many combinations of paper, plastic film, gelatin, egg albumin, silver, chemicals and colors in these 19th- and 20th-century
objects is such that they require sophisticated and expensive
treatment by photographic conservation specialists when they
have become damaged or decayed. These materials are
particularly vulnerable to moisture of any sort and unstable
climate. Twentieth-century colored photographic prints and
negatives are particularly vulnerable to light. All require
extra care.

Much has been and is still being written on conservation of photographic materials (see bibliography). Fortunately there is a primary source of sound reliable information on photographic conservation--The Technical and
Education Center of Graphic Arts, Rochester Institute of
Technology, Rochester, New York. There the university
faculty have recourse to the industrial resources in the city
to complement their own knowledge and expertise. Libraries
can rely with confidence on information in PhotographiConservation, a forum on photographic preservation and restoration published four times a year by the Center. The Center's occasional publications, and those monographs the
Center endorses on special aspects of photography and the
various photographic processes beginning with the daguerreo-
type can always be regarded as the best information available on that subject at the time of their publication. All
conservation librarians should have the Center's two most
recent bibliographies[22] by their desk at all times.

Although the Center of the Graphic Arts in Rochester
should be regarded as the clearinghouse for information on
photographic conservation in the United States, there have
been important publications on care of photographic materials
published elsewhere. This is acknowledged by their inclusion
in the bibliographies released by RIT. Among these are
Robert Weinstein's and Larry Booth's 1977 treatise on the
care of historic photographs;[23] the Eastman Kodak Company's
Preservation of Photographs;[24] and Henry Wilhelm's numerous publications on black and white and color photos, two of
which were presented at the 1978 conservation symposium at
Drake University in Iowa and published in the proceedings of
that meeting. [25, 26]

The preservation of motion picture and TV film,
which for at least twenty years has been practically all in
color, is more difficult than still photographs. Providing
a stable climate, preferably in cold storage, and separating
nitrate film are about all librarians and archivists can do
at this time. The immensity of the problem in trying to
maintain a film and television (film) archive on a national
scale, the astronomical costs involved and the technical difficulties were presented to the Royal Society of Arts in
London in March 1981 by the Director, British Film Institute. 27 The facts, which are equally applicable to any film
archive in the United States, are discouraging. There are
many problems still to be resolved. For the present, general guidance for motion picture and TV film preservation
is available from the Library of Congress. 28 Suggestions
for international cooperation in this matter were made at
the September-October 1980 Unesco meeting in Belgrade. 29

Microforms

Silver halide microfilm and microfiche, being black and
white images, are not as fugitive as color film; but these
polymer-based films (and magnetic tapes) which are making
such deep inroads into the domain so long ruled by paper
are vulnerable to temperature and humidity fluctuations,
sulfur dioxide and nitrous oxide in polluted air, and microbiological attacks by mold and fungus. They are also subject to hydrolysis by water. Because the rate of accumulation of these films and tapes is so high that recopying at
regular intervals (for preservation of the information) will
soon be prohibitively expensive, the National Archives has
commissioned the National Bureau of Standards to begin research on how microfilm and magnetic tape deteriorate and
how much material can be saved. When completed this study
will benefit all libraries and archives. Until that time custodians of these materials must concentrate on prevention of
damage by providing good storage, if possible, in a climate-
controlled environment as recommended by the Eastman Kodak
Company. 30 These plastics are different and they must be
used wisely and with care. For instance, microfilming
brittle books is less expensive "than any form of physical
treatment thus far available, [but] it is by no means
cheap.... For these reasons it seems vital to avoid un-
necessary duplication of original filming efforts. "18 Microfilm in addition to its importance in replication of worn-out
materials reduces the need to handle materials that are im-

portant as objects. It saves space and is the only sensible
method at this time to maintain newspaper collections.

    Microfilm services are available from publishing
houses, local commercial service agencies, and nonprofit
agencies such as the Northeast Document Conservation Center. The film used by all is the same; but the end product
differs in cost and quality because of the different degrees
of care used in preparing raw materials for copying, the
photography, and the processing of the exposed film. The
preparation of materials for microfilming for libraries and
archives often takes more time than filming and processing
the exposed film combined. In filming, the camera's aper-
ture size and shutter speed are fixed and the camera is adjusted for light intensity, focus, and image size. In commercial microfilming single settings are sometimes used for
light intensity and focus to save time--often with dire results. Preservation microfilming requires that each shot be
adjusted for light intensity to insure optimum background
density that influences resolution which is also affected by
focus, lens quality, vibration, and film quality. The focus
can be set for any one job if all the shots are through glass,
but this reduces output by 25-30 percent. Decreasing light
darkens the image on the film to get more detail from colored items and for maps with fine line delineations of topog-
raphy elevations, shore lines, water depth, etc. Processing
after filming requires development of the film with strictly
controlled temperatures and machine speed, plus careful
control of the hypo fixing agent, hypo remover, and final
washing. Quality control after processing requires a check
of each image (frame) for clarity and to see that the sequence of images in the film matches the sequence of pages
in the original.

    The difference between archival microfilming and
preservation microfilming is that archival microfilming stip-
ulates: a) the use of high quality film, with b) carefully
controlled processing, and c) excellent storage conditions
for the finished film. Preservation microfilming requires
all that plus d) much attention to the preparation for filming
(targeting, collation, arrangement and organization of material), and e) minute attention to image quality including many
test exposures. It is possible to do high quality microfilming meeting all the presently prescribed standards and specifications for archival filming and end up with unreadable
images or unusable data on the film if steps d) and e) are
neglected.

The finest microfilming available is wasted if the
finished product (master negatives and security positives) is
not kept in a carefully controlled (archival storage) environment. That requires stable temperature and relative humidity (65° F and 40%RH) day and night year-round; with filtered
air and in constant darkness. All of the care expended in
preparation, filming, processing, and quality control is for
nought if the storage of the finished film is neglected. After that the single most critical factor is the condition of the
original documents. This can be controlled to a certain extent in filming technique, but it is a major cost factor in
the overall operation. Roy Engelbretson wisely observes
that microfilming is not a cure-all and that it can be much
too costly unless used with some discretion. [31] He suggests
that these factors always be kept in mind in making decisions
in regard to the use of it: a) space saving--weigh cost of
space saved against cost of the microfilm; b) security; c)
speed and convenience of retrieval; d) low cost distribution;
e) costs in comparison to other means of preserving deteriorated records; f) costs of preparing the data for the actual
filming; g) difficulty in photography (wide variations in physical characteristics of the raw material); h) the size of the
record series; i) reference requirements (readers and reader printers). Microfilming makes storage, retrieval, and
speedy dissemination of great quantities of records possible
with efficiency and economy. It is probably the best answer
for brittle books and newspaper collections. In other instances, it may or may not be--that is a management decision.

Security

Fire prevention and provisions for security from theft and
vandalism, usually considered under the general category of
disaster, are also preventive conservation. Money spent
for fire, flood, and intruder warning systems often prevents
loss or damage that would have otherwise occurred. Much
has been published on security in libraries and archives (see
bibliography). We suggest Timothy Walch's basic manual
Archives and Manuscripts: Security[32] as a starting text for
librarians as well as archivists.

In-House Training and Indoctrination

The Conservation Program at Stanford University Library[33]
includes education of staff, faculty and other users, as an

important part of the overall preservation effort. This preventive conservation includes slide/tape and video programs
about conservation efforts; assembling exhibits; writing articles for the University's Library Bulletin; giving informal
talks; and organizing meetings on the campus at which conservation specialists are invited to speak.

Of particular interest are these information aids used
at Stanford:

a) A User's Guide to the Conservation of Library Mate-
     rials (booklet)
b) a conservation bookmark
c) a "brittle book" label for books that may not be
     photocopied
d) an "extreme care" label for books that are marginal
     for photocopying
e) staff guides on deacidification, water damage, insect
     damage, exhibits, encapsulation, leather dressing,
     and cleaning library materials
f) instructions for proper photocopying techniques that
     are prominently displayed near all copy machines

Elsewhere librarians have prepared 35mm slide/tape
cassettes and video tape presentations on preventive conservation measures (see bibliography). One particularly good
example is the slide/tape kit Preservation of Library Materials prepared by the Preservation of Library Materials
Project Committee, Memorial Library, University of Wisconsin, Madison. This presentation on care and handling of
books in general and in the stacks in particular is applicable
to all types of library materials.

Cooperation in Preventive Conservation

In her conservative analysis of the trend toward regional
conservation services, Hilda Bohem, Department of Special
Collections, University Research Library, University of
California, Los Angeles makes a very strong case for preventive conservation by what she terms "good library keeping."[34] In her opinion, librarians, while waiting for regional cooperative conservation programs to solve some of
their mutual problems, "need a service which can take over
the supervisory jobs which we cannot perform in our libraries for lack of time." She recommends a regional con-

servation administrator who would concentrate on stack
cleaning by trained crews, disinfecting, inspection of buildings and repairs as necessary, environment control engineering advice, and all other good housekeeping and maintenance chores that create an environment in which the conditions which exacerbate book decay are abated. In developing her thesis, which she does well, Bohem very effectively
demonstrates the importance of housekeeping and prevention
of damage. We do wish that she had carried the idea one
step further with a flat statement, that until they can get
specialists for conservation maintenance, librarians as
managers must find time to manage that aspect of running
their libraries.

References

1.   Barr, Pelham. "Book Conservation and University Li-
     brary Administration," College and Research Li-
     braries 7:214-219, 1946.

2.   Buck, Richard D. "On Conservation," Museum News
     52(1):15-16, 1973.

3.   Patterson, Robert H. "Organizing for Conservation,"
     Library Journal 104:1116-19, May 15, 1979.

4.   Schnare, Robert E., Jr. "How to Handle Your Deteri-
     orating Book Collections from an Administrative
     Point of View," The Library Scene 8(3):12-13, 1979.

5.   Morrow, Carolyn Clark. A Conservation Policy State-
     ment for Research Libraries. Urbana: University
     of Illinois, Graduate School of Library Science,
     1979.

6.   Cunha, George M. What an Institution Can Do to Sur-
     vey Its Conservation Needs. New York: New York
     Library Assn, 1979.

7.   Lowell, Howard P. Planning for Library Conservation:
     A Needs Assessment Manual. Denver: Colorado
     State Library, 1981.

8.   SAA Basic Archival Conservation Program Conservation
     Self Study. Chicago: Society of American Archiv-
     ists, 1982.

9. Feilden, Bernard. An Introduction to Conservation of
    Cultural Property. Rome: ICCROM, 1979.

10. Darling, Pamela W. "Doing Preservation With or
    Without Money," Oklahoma Librarian 30(4):20-26,
    1980.

    _____. "A Local Preservation Program--Where to
    Start," Library Journal 101:2343-47, Nov. 15, 1976.

11. "Movable Compact Shelving: A Survey of U.S. Sup-
    pliers and Library Users," Library Technology Re-
    ports 17(1):1981.

12. Rutstein, Joel S. Preservation and Collection Develop-
    ment: Establishing the Connection. A paper pre-
    sented at the ACRL National Conference, Minneap-
    olis, October 1981.

13. Buchanan, S. and S. Coleman. Deterioration Survey
    of the Stanford University Libraries Green Library
    Stack Collection. Stanford, California: Stanford
    University Libraries, 1980.

14. Darling, Pamela (ed.). The Preservation of Library
    Materials: A Cul Handbook. New York: Columbia
    University Libraries, 1980.

15. Preservation of Library Materials Kit #35. Washing-
    ington: Systems and Procedures Exchange Center,
    Association of Research Libraries, 1977.

16. Standard for Library Binding. Boston: The Library
    Binding Institute, 1981.

17. American Library Assn, Bookbinding Committee "Mini-
    mum Specifications for Binding Lesser Used Materi-
    als," ALA Bulletin 52(1):51-53, 1958.

18. Banks, Paul. "The Preservation of Library Materials,"
    Encyclopedia of Library and Information Science,
    Vol. 23. New York: Marcel Dekker, 1978. This
    essay is available as a reprint from the Newberry
    Library, Chicago.

19. DeCandido, Robert. "Preservation Treatments Avail-
    able to Librarians," The Library Scene 8(1):4-6,
    1979.

20. Dean, John. "Growth Control in the Research Li-
     brary," Steady State, Zero Growth and the Aca-
     demic Library. C. Sleele (ed.). Hamden: Lin-
     net, 1978.

21. Cunha, G. M. and D. G. Conservation of Library Ma-
     terials. Metuchen, New Jersey: Scarecrow Press,
     1971 (pp. 116+).

22. Knittel, Patricia (ed.). A Selected Bibliography on
     Photographic Conservation Jan. 1975--Dec. 1980.
     Rochester: Rochester Institute of Technology, 1980.
     Barger, M. Susan (comp.). Bibliography of Photo-
     graphic Processes in Use Before 1880: Their Mate-
     rials, Processing and Conservation. Rochester:
     Rochester Institute of Technology, 1980.

23. Weinstein, R. A. and L. Booth. Collection, Use and
     Care of Historical Photographs. Nashville: Amer-
     ican Association for State and Local History, 1977.

24. Preservation of Photographs. Rochester, N. Y. : East-
     man Kodak Company, 1979. (Kodak Publication #f-
     30).

25. Wilhelm, Henry. "Preservation of Black and White
     Photographs," Preserving Your Historical Records.
     Toby Fishbein and Alan Perry (eds.). Kansas
     City: Federal Archives and Records Center, 1980.

26. _____. "Stability and Preservation of Color Photo-
     graphs," ibid.

27. Smith, Anthony. "Mixing Chemistry with Culture--
     Preserving Film and Television," Royal Society of
     Arts Journal 129(5299):423-434, 1981.

28. Write to Motion Picture Broadcasting and Recorded
     Sound Division, The Library of Congress, Washing-
     ton, D. C.

29. Recommendations for the Safeguarding and Preservation
     of Moving Images. Paris, Unesco, 1980. Adopted
     by the General Conference of Unesco at its 21st
     session, Belgrade, September/October 1980.

30. Storage and Preservation of Microfilm. Rochester,

New York: Eastman Kodak Co. , 1976 (Kodak
Pamphlet D-31).

31.   Engelbretson, Roy. "Microfilming in South Dakota's
       Records Management Program," National Preserva-
       tion Report 1(1):10-15, 1979. Washington: National
       Preservation Program Office, Library of Congress.

32.   Walch, Timothy. Archives and Manuscripts: Security.
       Chicago: Society of American Archivists, 1977.

33.   Buchanan, Sally. "The Conservation Program at Stan-
       ford University Library," Conservation Administra-
       tion News No. 7, June 1981.

34.   Bohem, Hilda. "Regional Conservation Services: What
       can we do for ourselves?" Library Journal 104:
       1428-31, July 1979.

Chapter VII

DISASTERS

"Disaster--an event whose time is unexpected and
whose consequences are seriously destructive. "
--Hilda Bohem[10]

Unquestionably one of the most satisfying developments in conservation management in the 1970s was the
realization that although disasters occur with distressing
frequency the effects of these misfortunes can often be
minimized and recovery expedited by sensible advance planning. More than in any other area of conservation collection managers have assumed leadership in this most important aspect of their work.

After seminars and workshops in disaster control
throughout the country, similar to that in the Denver area
in June 1981,[1] many of the participants have returned home
to prepare plans for their own establishments[2] and to organize task forces for regional cooperation, or at the state
level in disaster control.[3]

The frequency and variety of disasters is awesome.
No one, even those in new buildings of modern construction,
is completely safe from these unwanted natural or man-made
misfortunes. Walter Brahm in a 1978 study for Case Western Reserve University[4] reported that in Ohio alone from
1968 to 1973 there were fifty major disasters (ten per
year). The requirement then is to benefit from the experiences of those who have had such calamities and plan accordingly.

Categories of Disasters

Disasters can be classified in four categories--Acts of God,
accidents, vandalism, and catastrophes resulting from human

error.   Acts of God include earthquakes often followed by
holocaust; hurricanes with great tides and torrential rains;
tornadoes and cyclones with their violent destructive winds;
and rivers overflowing their banks during spring floods.
Examples are the hurricane that caused so much havoc at
the University of Corpus Christi in 1970; Hurricane Agnes
that devastated the Corning Museum of Glass with its important library on the history of glass in 1972; Hurricanes
David and Frederick that ripped across the Gulf and Atlantic
Coasts from Mississippi to North Carolina in September
1979 and the tornado that flattened the Museum of Aviation
History in Windsor, Connecticut in October 1979.   The great
San Francisco fire in 1906 was the aftermath of an earthquake.   The Mississippi River and its tributaries in the
Spring of 1979 flooded hundreds of square miles threatening
all the libraries and records centers in the area and seri-
ously damaging the Fish and Game Records Repository in
Jackson.   Communities in the great forested areas of the
Northwest are threatened almost annually by conflagrations
that can go on for weeks.

        Disastrous library fires have been the result of fur-
nace room accidents or defective electric circuits in older
buildings.   Destruction by combustion, plus the soot and
smoke damage from even a minor blaze, could bankrupt a
small community library.   In most cases the water from
firemen's hoses does more damage than the flames quenched
by that water.

        Water damage often requiring tens of thousands of
dollars for repair and restoration is sometimes caused by
plumbing failures occurring in areas of the library often
remote from the book stacks and other storage areas.   The
damage done by malfunctioning sprinkler and air conditioning
systems can be even worse.   Basement stack areas have
been filled to a depth of six to ten feet by ground water entering through cracks in the building foundation or by ruptured water pipes.   Melting snow and torrential rains find
their way into shelves of books in the upper levels of libraries through aged roofs.

        The ingenuity of vandals has been demonstrated by
their tampering with sprinkler systems, air conditioning mechanisms, fire mains, and plumbing facilities to release
water on books and artifacts in libraries.   Vandalism by
fire is not only the work of arsonists, such as at the Federal Records Repository in St. Louis in 1973.   Malefactors

have been known to destroy smaller libraries in residential
communities by stuffing balled-up newspapers in book-return
slots and then igniting the paper by dropping lighted matches
into the slot on top of the newsprint. War damage, the ultimate in vandalism, is as old as history. We can only hope
that we shall be spared such catastrophes in the future.

Vandalism by theft in libraries can be controlled to
a certain extent by the use of sophisticated intruder alarm
and book detection systems. Theft of documents, on the
other hand, is difficult to eliminate except by inventorying
boxes and file folders before and after each use. This type
of disaster, while less dramatic than raging fires and
floods, can be just as costly in material loss.

Disasters--because of oversight on the part of those
working in and about libraries; or even those not associated
in any way with the day-to-day operation of libraries, archives, and other record repositories--which should be controllable are usually not. The great flood of Florence in
1966 might not have happened if the flood gates in the Arno
River above the city had been operated with more skill when
the water first began to rise. Twice in the last ten years
overzealous workmen, digging with earth-moving machinery
during the construction of additions to libraries in Texas and
California, have ruptured water mains releasing tens of
thousands of gallons of water into basement stacks of the
existing structures. Clogged roof drains and storm sewers
can cause much grief when backed-up water finds its way
into attic and basement storage areas.

The probability of cataclysms such as that at Florence, the San Francisco Earthquake and the Great Chicago
Fire is reasonably remote, but the probability of lesser but
equally calamitous disasters to the institutions concerned is
higher than most managers realize. The list is horrendous.
The fact that must be accepted by librarians and others responsible for safeguarding the records of our heritage is
that ... "it can happen to you." When it does, in addition
to the threat of loss of information in books and other collections in a library, there are the inescapable recovery
costs which are seldom fully regained from insurance policies in those instances when the collections are "protected"
by insurance. Disasters can result in loss of jobs, sometimes personal injury, and even loss of life. A major
calamity could require millions of dollars for the repair and
restoration of the collections over and above the costs for

HYPOTHETICAL COSTS FOR
RESTORING 100,000 LIBRARY VOLUMES DAMAGED BY FIRE OR FLOOD

Category of Restoration	Number of Books	%	Cost per Book	Dollars Required
Discard	10,000	10	----	----
Replacement	20,000	20	$ 10.00	$ 200,000
Restoration				
Minimum	10,000	10	$ 1.00	$ 10,000
Intermediate	50,000	50	$ 10.00	$ 500,000
Complete	10,000	10	$500.00	$5,000,000
			TOTAL COSTS	$5,710,000

Source: Fischer, David J. "Problems Encountered, Hurricane AGNES Flood, June 23, 1972 at Corning, New York" in Conservation Administration, Robert Morrison, ed., New England Document Conservation Center, 1975.

Figure 5.

building repair. Even a minor accident could result in the necessity for spending hundreds if not thousands of dollars for cleanup alone. The chart (Figure 5) of estimated costs for the recovery of books (building repair not included) in a fire- or water-damaged library of 100,000 volumes was prepared by those primarily concerned with the salvage of the books in the Corning Museum of Glass Library of the History of Glass after Hurricane Agnes in 1972. This compilation was based on the costs for labor and materials in 1973. Present day charges will almost double the figure shown. These estimates can be scaled up or down to predict the funds that would be required for a recovery from a major disaster in any larger or smaller establishment.

Disaster Prevention

Safeguarding collections begins with housekeeping, building maintenance, fire protection, and protection from theft and vandalism. Included in the ample literature on fire protection is John Morris's Managing the Library Fire Risk[5] and the American Library Association's Protecting the Library and Its Resources,[6] both of which should be used for guidance in evaluating the fire protection capability of any library.

Security from theft and vandalism has also been given much attention in the last five years, and there is considerable literature on this subject to assist librarians in investigating this matter in their own establishments. Timothy Walch's important book, Archives and Manuscripts: Security,[7] written for archivists but equally useful for librarians, discusses many aspects of building and collection security. It is recommended as a point of departure for any study of this aspect of conservation management, as is Rudolph Bold's essays on security systems.[8]

Over and above the importance of making the library a clean and orderly place in which to work, good housekeeping prevents the accumulation in attics, basements, storerooms and utility rooms of flammable debris and combustible surplus books, newsprint, and other materials waiting to be discarded. It should be the responsibility of a senior member of every staff to make a weekly inspection of the building from cellar to attic to insure good housekeeping. In these inspections one should look particularly for cleaning fluids and other volatile solvents used by maintenance per-

sonnel, to insure that they are kept in safety cans for immediate use and outside solvent storage cabinets for bulk supplies.

The director or a senior assistant in cooperation
with the plant maintenance supervisor should establish programs for:

a)   Periodic inspections and testing of intruder alarms,
     heat or smoke sensors and fire-quenching systems
     if they are in the building.
b)   Annual inspections of the building's foundation for
     cracks or breaks in the walls and floor.
c)   Spring and Fall inspections of the roof for water
     tightness, loose slates or shingles, and the bonding
     of flashings around chimneys and roof vents.
d)   Annual inspections of all electrical wiring, plumbing,
     and steam and hot water pipes with emphasis on the
     condition of air conditioners and sprinkler system
     pipes and fittings.
e)   Monthly inspections of roof drains and gutters, drains
     in the cellar and storm drains outside the building to
     see if they are free of debris and free flowing.

If basement spaces are used for book stacks, the library staff should reexamine shelving policies to see if the
basement rooms can be used for less valuable books, rather
than the older infrequently used but important materials of
permanent value that are so often relegated to these areas.
In any case every effort should be made to rearrange the
shelving so that at least the lower shelves in each tier remain empty.

Disaster Plans

The best way to handle disasters is to assume that they can
and probably will happen to you and plan accordingly. Every
library, archives, historical society, and public records'
repository must have a disaster plan. These plans should
include a disaster prevention section (pre-disaster preparedness) and a disaster action section--the first to prevent or
minimize damage when trouble is imminent and the second
to control the salvage operations after the event. Some
thought might also be given to long-range recovery operations
extending over a period of up to twenty years. Repair and
restoration of the Magliabechi and Palatina collections has

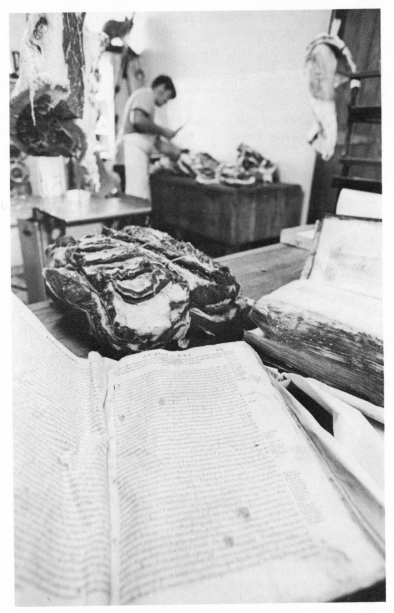

Figure 6.   Flood Damage, Corning Museum of Glass Library.

been going on in the Biblioteca Nazionale Centrale in Florence since 1966 and will continue for at least another decade.

Disaster Prevention Plan

In general terms the prevention section of a disaster plan
should include.

- a) Assumptions of what could happen--that is a list of
  all possible causes for damage from external and internal sources.
- b) A summary of measures for the early detection of
  every type of damage that might take place.
- c) Provisions for early warning of an impending disaster
  to all concerned.
- d) The organization of a disaster prevention team (DPT)
  by job description, rather than individuals, that will
  be activated when great storms, floods, or other
  trouble is predicted.
- e) The authority of the head of the DPT over other members of the team and in relation to various departments of the library (and/or the college or university
  if applicable).
- f) Written guidelines to prevent or minimize all possible
  cause for damage and to establish responsibility.
- g) Lists of supplies and suppliers in the local area and
  elsewhere in the event the local sources are put out
  of operation.
- h) Location of quick-freeze establishments and sources
  for refrigerator trucks and other automotive equipment.
- i) Lists of individuals and agencies to whom you can
  turn for help.
- j) List of telephone numbers and addresses for each individual currently on the DPT and alternates.

Disaster Recovery Plan

The broad requirements for the disaster recovery section of
a disaster plan are to provide guidance for the Disaster Recovery Team (DRT), the membership of which might or
might not correspond with the membership of the DPT.
These instructions should include:

- a) The organization of the DRT by job description rather
  than individuals.

Psalm of the Center

Conservation is my destiny.
I will not reshelve.
It treateth my paper for strong acids.
It restoreth my scrolls.
It draggeth me into chemistry,
for my own good.

Yea, though I splash thru the waters
of soda and paste,
I will begrudge no custodian.
They provideth me a bench
in the presence of history,
and grindeth my nose on its wheel.

Surely bad molds and bugs shall follow me
all the days of my life
and I shall dwell in the house of old books
forever.

Robert C. Morrison, Jr.
New England Document
Conservation Center, 1977

Figure 7.

b)   Responsibilities of each member of the DRT after the
     disaster has happened.
c)   Authority of the head of the DRT with respect to oth-
     ers on the team and in relation to other departments
     of the library (and the college or university if appli-
     cable).
d)   Priorities for salvage of the various collections and
     categories of materials in the library.
e)   Written step-by-step procedures for each salvage op-
     eration.
f)   Instructions for the supervision of volunteers includ-
     ing provisions for their safety.
g)   Specific location within the building of each major
     collection and each category of material with stack
     diagrams.
h)   List of individuals and establishments to whom you
     can turn for help.
i)   Location of quick-freeze establishments and sources
     for refrigerator trucks and other automotive equip-
     ment.
j)   Location of other buildings on the campus (or in the
     community) that can be designated as on-scene treat-
     ment sites (i. e. gymnasiums, chemistry laboratories,
     armories, etc.).
k)   Lists of supplies and suppliers in the local area and
     elsewhere.

     The American Association for State and Local His-
tory's bibliography on emergency preparedness for museums,
historic sites and archives[9] which should be retitled to include libraries, should be at every collection manager's
desk.   The bibliography Appendix M in this book, based on
experience from two disasters within a brief time at Cornell
University Libraries and reprinted with the permission of
compiler Richard Strassberg, Cornell University archivist,
will give an idea of the scope of the literature available for
guidance.   It is further suggested that those responsible for
preparing disaster plans also obtain and examine plans prepared by conservation committees at:

a)   The University of California[10]
b)   New Jersey State Library[11]
c)   The University of Michigan[12]
d)   Tulane University[13]

     These are suggested for review because they show
four different approaches to the problem.   It is mandatory

to remember, however, that they are for general guidance only. Every establishment is unique, requiring its own plans based on probable external threats in its geographical area, as well as the institution's particular vulnerabilities due to the age and construction features of the building, the location of the building relative to the seacoast and/or river-beds, the size and characteristics of the collections, even the number of staff personnel and their experience. See Appendix K for more factors to consider in disaster planning.

Disaster Recovery Plans implemented by well-organized and well-trained Disaster Recovery Teams will expedite retrieval by having pre-established priorities for salvage of various categories of materials. Lists of salvage materials and locations should be prepared in advance where they are available. Detailed guidelines should be written for every anticipated recovery operation. Those replaceable reference materials, periodicals, newspaper collections, etc., that are cheaper to write off than to salvage should be identified. These actions will eliminate much wasted effort and minimize further damage to already sodden and/or charred materials by well meaning, but overzealous volunteers, if not by the institution's own maintenance personnel, who do not see the recovery problem from the librarian's point of view.

Cooperative Disaster Planning

It is conceded that the establishment of Disaster Action Teams (DAT) for prevention and recovery are feasible only in college and university libraries and larger public libraries in which there are a number of librarians and people from other administrative departments from which to draw the personnel and skills needed. Smaller establishments with only a few employees need not be denied the benefits of DATs if they will pool their resources in a local area to provide "on call" the Recovery Director and his team of assistants, plus the electrician, plumber, carpenter, pest controller, chemist, professional conservator, mycologist, etc., all of whose services will be needed at one time or another. It is suggested that the organization of Regional Disaster Assistance Teams is an appropriate matter for consideration by city, state, and regional associations; or as has been done in Kentucky by the State Department for Library and Archives.[14]

Disaster Recovery

Regardless of how well plans have been made or how well
they have been carried out, when a disaster strikes there
invariably is destruction of some sort that requires quick
action to minimize water damage. Immediate freeze stabilization, when there are great numbers of wet volumes, followed by freeze drying at a later time, is now regarded as
the most effective recovery tactic when libraries have been
inundated by flood waters, drenched by great storms, or
made sodden by other causes including firemen's hoses.
Robert DeCandido's brief description of procedures for salvaging by freezing wet books in Library Scene[15] is very
good.   Sally Buchanan's discourse on fire and water damage
in Oklahoma Librarian[16] is more complete.   Phillip Leighton's book length report[17] on all of the ramifications in
connection with the salvage of the tens of thousands of water
saturated books in the basement of the Meyer Library at
Stanford University in 1978 is unquestionably the most complete critical analysis, including the costs, of a disaster
recovery operation that has been made.

Freeze Stabilization

Because of the unquestionable importance of freeze stabilization (and ultimately freeze drying) of wet volumes after a
fire or flood, all custodians of bulky records should keep
readily available, at home as well as in their offices, the
addresses of trucking firms operating refrigerator vans, and
commercial cold storage warehouses in which the wet volumes can be quickly frozen after delivery by the trucks.   It
would be wise to become acquainted with the management in
those establishments now to make them aware of your potential needs.   There will be no time to search for sources of
assistance and negotiate terms when wet volumes are becoming infested with mold (within 48 hours).   These busi-
nessmen will often be willing to donate the use of their
services and facilities when made aware of the facts, particularly when it is made clear that they will be rewarded
by favorable publicity for such public service.

Freeze Drying

Once books and other bulky records are stabilized by freezing, the pressure is off and there is time to investigate the

Figure 8.   Flood damage, Corning Museum of Glass Library.

availability of research and/or industrial vacuum chambers
for freeze drying.   Some of these establishments in the
past have been willing to donate the use of this sophisticated
and costly equipment and the time of the engineers and technicians to operate it. [18], [19]   Others do it for a fee. [20], [21]

The National Fire Protection Association's publications on fire prevention[22-25] are excellent, but planners
should also rely heavily on reports of the actual experiences of others in recovery from fire damage.   Very useful are recommendations by R. H. Hamilton, [26] J. S. Still, [27]
and Adelaide Minogue. [28]

It is seldom that a library will only have to recover
partially burned or scorched volumes.   Usually when it is
permissable to enter a building after a fire everything that
has been burned or scorched will have been wet as well by
the quenching of the fire.   The exceptions are when the
building was protected by a carbon dioxide system or one
of the extremely effective systems using the halogenated
flame extinguishing agent, "HALON."   In the latter case because of the extreme efficiency of the freon fire quenching,
the burn damage will be minimal.

Accidents to Personnel

Two major universities that have carried their disaster preparedness plans beyond the salvage of materials to include
protection from (or response to) the many accidents that
can happen to people in libraries are Cornell University[29]
and the University of Colorado at Boulder. [30]   These two
plans include instructions for reaction to insect and animal
bites, drug and psychiatric problems, bomb threats, etc.
in addition to fire, flooding, and windstorm.   There are
undoubtedly many more such emergency directives in colleges and universities throughout the country.   Librarians
who have not anticipated such contingencies should carefully
consider all the possibilities of personnel casualties on
their premises and what should be done when such mishaps
take place.

Federal Assistance

When the inevitable happens and there has been a catastro-
phe, there is the possibility of Federal Disaster Assistance.

Section 402, Public Law 93-288 authorizes Federal assistance for the restoration of public facilities which are damaged or destroyed by a major disaster.   Federal regulation
24 CFR 2205. 54(j) and the FDA Eligibility Handbook (3300. 6
Rev) pages 5-51 provide that such assistance includes related office equipment and supplies, library books, and publications.   Such assistance is available following a request
by the Governor of the affected state and a declaration of a
major disaster by the President. [31]

References

1.   Moon, Myra J.   "A Report of the Colorado Disaster
        Prevention and Preparedness Workshop," Colorado
        Libraries 7(3):39-43, 1981.

2.   Some good examples are:

        a)   The Greater Cincinnati Library Consortium/
              Dayton-Miami Valley Consortium's Disaster Pre-
              paredness Task Force.

        b)   The Task Force to Prepare a Preservation
              Maintenance and Disaster Preparedness Manual
              for the MIT Libraries.

        c)   The Kentucky Council on Archives Emergency
              Task Force Committee's studies.

3.   a)   Harms, R. H. , F. L. Honhart and D. J. Olson.
              A Program for Disaster Response in Michigan.
              East Lansing: Michigan Archival Assn, 1981.

        b)   Patterson, Robert H.   "Wyoming DRAT," (Dis-
              aster Recovery Assistance Team) Colorado Li-
              braries 7(2):26-36, 1981.

        c)   Porter, Barry L.   Iowa Statewide Disaster Re-
              covery Plan for Libraries.   Des Moines: State
              Library Commission of Iowa, 1981.

        d)   Duff, Jeffrey M.   Kentucky Disaster Plan.
              Frankfort: Department for Library and Ar-
              chives, 1981.

        e)   Alexander, David.   "Regional Disaster Prepared-

ness and Recovery," Colorado Libraries 7(3):33-
38, 1981.

4. Brahm, Walter. An Appraisal of the Need for Con-
    servation Facilities and Services by Ohio Libraries.
    Cleveland, Ohio: Case Western Reserve University,
    1978.

5. Morris, John. Managing the Library Fire Risk.
    Berkeley: University of California, Office of Insur-
    ance and Risk Management, 1981.

6. Protecting the Library and Its Resources. Chicago:
    The American Library Assn, 1963.

7. Walch, Timothy. Archives and Manuscripts: Security.
    Chicago: Society of American Archivists, 1977.

8. Bold, Rudolph. "Sensoring Public Libraries--A Secur-
    ity Primer," Wilson Library Bulletin 53(1):71-73,
    1978.

9. Hunter, J. E. Emergency Preparedness for Museums,
    Historical Sites and Archives: An Annotated Bib-
    liography. Nashville: American Association for
    State and Local History, Technical Leaflet #114.

10. Bohem, Hilda. Disaster and Disaster Preparedness.
    Berkeley: University of California, 1978.

11. New Jersey State Library Disaster Preparedness Plan.
    Trenton, N. J.: Bureau of Archives and History,
    1980.

12. Craven, James and Ann Flowers. Disaster Plan for
    the Bentley Library. Ann Arbor: University of
    Michigan Library, 1979.

13. Meneray, Wilbur E. Tulane University Disaster Plan.
    New Orleans: Tulane University Library Depart-
    ment, 1977.

14. On July 14, 1981 James A. Nelson, Kentucky State Li-
    brarian, issued this policy memorandum: "Effective
    immediately it shall be the policy of this agency that
    our disaster assistance capability is available to any
    public or private establishment within the state where
    there are important records of Kentucky's heritage."

15. DeCandido, Robert. "Preserving Our Library Materials," Library Scene 8(3):6-8, 1979.

16. Buchanan, Sally. "Disaster Prevention and Action," Oklahoma Librarian 30(4):35-41, 1980.

17. Leighton, Phillip D. Disasters: Prevention and Coping. Stanford: Stanford University Library, 1981.

18. "Lockheed saves soggy records--again," Lockheed Life 5(2):3, 1981. Report on the salvage of Spalding County, Georgia Courthouse records in the Lockheed vacuum chamber in their Marietta, Georgia plant.

19. "Millions of Records Salvaged by Freeze Drying Process," Library Journal 98(21):3491, 1973. A report on the recovery of the St. Louis Federal Records Center Materials.

20. Water Damage Reclamation Service, McDonald Aircraft Company, Dept. 256, BLD. 702, Post L140, P.O. Box 516, St. Louis, MO 63166.

21. American Freeze-Dry, Inc., 411 White Horse Pike, Audubon, N.J. 08106.

22. Protection of Library Collections. Boston: National Fire Protection Assn, 1975. NFPA No. 910.

23. Protection of Records. Boston: National Fire Protection Assn, 1975. NFPA No. 232.

24. Manual of Fire Protection for Archives and Records Centers. Boston: National Fire Protection Assn, 1979. NFPA No. 232 AM.

25. McKinnon, G.P. (ed.). Fire Protection Handbook. Boston: National Fire Protection Assn, 1976.

26. Hamilton, R.M. "The Library of Parliament Fire," American Archivist 16(2):141-144, 1953.

27. Still, J.S. "Library Fires and Salvage Methods," American Archivist 16(2):145-153, 1953.

28. Minogue, A.E. "Treatment of Fire and Water Damaged Records," American Archivist (1):17-25, 1966.

29.   Emergency Manual.   Ithaca, New York: Cornell Uni-
       versity Libraries, 1976.

30.   Emergency Definitions.   Boulder: University of Colo-
       rado Libraries, 1979.

31.   Letter from office of the Administrator, Office of
       Housing and Urban Development, Federal Disaster
       Assistance Administration to Director, New England
       Document Conservation Center dated December 14,
       1978.

Chapter VIII

IN-HOUSE CONSERVATION--TREATMENT

A great deal of the treatment necessary to repair damaged materials can be done in-house by the staff, or students and volunteers working under the direction of the staff, if work space is available and a modest sum is invested in equipment and supplies. It is not unrealistic to state that as much as eighty percent of the work that has to be done (exclusive of commercial binding) could be accomplished by careful and dedicated workers who are provided with necessary tools and suitable working conditions--and are well supervised. That eighty percent would not include hand bookbinding and binding restoration; or treatment of illuminated book pages, parchment and vellum scrolls, hand colored antique maps, watercolor paintings, colored prints and drawings, and other works of art on paper in library collections. They belong in the twenty percent category that can only be properly treated by book binders and paper conservators who have had extensive training and long experience. The eighty percent category includes moderately damaged case-bound books in circulating libraries; printed and written documents; some black and white prints; general map collections; and some photographic materials that make up the bulk of collections. The treatments that could be stipulated (all or in part) by the person in charge of the in-house workshop for most black and white items include:

1. Removal of pressure sensitive tape
2. Cleaning
   Wet
   Dry
3. Deacidification
   Aqueous
   Nonaqueous
   Vapor phase

4. Mending and reinforcing
   Rag paper and paste mends
   With archival quality mending tapes
   Thermoplastic repair tissue mends
   Encapsulation of damaged or brittle flat paper
   Reinforcement of brittle paper with nylon webb
5. Cased book cover repairs
6. Making portfolios for pamphlets and documents
7. Making protective boxes for dilapidated books (We
   consider the cleaning and oiling of leather bound
   books to be a measure in preventive conservation programs.)
8. Cleaning and repackaging photographic materials
9. Removal of acid cardboard and/or wood backs from
   framed items
10. Leaf casting repairs for damaged paper

There is an abundance of instructions for this hands-
on conservation (see bibliography) including excellent printed
guidance from sources such as the Northeast Document Conservation Center,[1] the Library of Congress,[2] and Yale University Library.[3] There are also some exceedingly well-
done video tapes and slide/cassette combinations on these
basic treatments from the Smithsonian Institution[4] and the
Nebraska State Historical Society.[5] The Association of Research Libraries Spec Kit 70, Section 2[6] delves into actual
treatments that can be done in-house by people with only
basic training.

The major requirement is an understanding of what
can and should be done in-house and rigid in-house discipline
to insure that staff, students, and volunteers strictly follow
the technical instructions (printed or on tapes or slides)
provided by the supervising librarian. Pearl Berger, Assistant Librarian at the YIVO Institute for Jewish Research,
has written well on this subject[7] after a careful study of
many sources of information. It is her opinion that regardless of the arguments against in-house treatment of materials, "...the reality of the library world forces us to
counter them with some very practical considerations" (ibid.,
p. 1312).

Berger then goes on to describe, with good illustra-
tions, treatment she considers appropriate for use in a small
library preservation workshop--all of which is well done.
We cannot, however, agree with her position that deacidification and pressure sensitive tape removal should not be

done in-house. If those heinous tapes are not soon removed from paper and the paper embrittling acid neutralized, flat paper and book pages are doomed. Without tape removal and deacidification (on those materials important enough for long retention) most other in-house paper treatment is merely providing "deathbed care and funerary vestments for the about to be deceased."

At the beginning of any program it would be wise for those concerned to retain a professional consultant to help make the initial selection of materials for in-house and professional treatment. Such service is available on a day-to-day basis from the Northeast Document Conservation Center. [8] The names of other conservation consultants are available from the Guild of Book Workers, [9] the Society of American Archivists[10] and the American Institute for Conservation. [11]

Since this book is not intended to be a manual of conservation techniques, the following information and that in the Appendices is presented for general guidance only, and to suggest sources for specific information on techniques that are also listed in the bibliography.

Pressure Sensitive Tape Removal

The tens of millions of strips of this commercial tape used to "repair" torn book pages and flat paper in permanent collections will, if it has not happened already, first stain the paper, then obscure the printed or written words and finally chemically degrade the paper--sometimes with actual loss of the paper substance. Pressure sensitive tape strips must be removed from all library and archival materials that are not expendable. Most of these tape strips can be removed in-house with one or another of the solvents described in Appendix J. The Smithsonian Institution has for rent or sale a twenty minute video presentation on how actually to do it. [4]

Cleaning Paper

Although in some fields "dry cleaning" is considered to be the removal of soil and dirt with solvents--as clothes are cleaned in a laundry--in conservation dry cleaning, sometimes called surface cleaning, is the mechanical removal of surface soil with rubber erasers, ground art gum, wallpaper

cleaning plastic doughs, etc.   The processes used at the
Northeast Document Conservation Center are reprinted in
Appendix E by permission of Ann Russell, Director NEDCC.
See also the Smithsonian Institution's suggestions. [4]

Wet cleaning is washing of paper in hot, warm or
cold water to remove water soluble stains sometimes with
the use of soap or detergents.   Judith Hofenk-de Graaff at the
Central Research Laboratory for Objects of Art and Science,
Amsterdam includes explicit instructions for mechanical
cleaning and washing of paper in the Yearbook of Paper History 1980. [12]

Deacidification

In 1969 Richard Smith observed that little-used books will
remain intact on shelves long after their leaves are too
brittle to handle.   He also noted that permanence (low rate
of deterioration) is much more important than durability for
infrequently used books and that the best time to preserve
books is when they are new.   The acid deterioration of paper must be curbed, preferably by control of the manufacturing process, but also on the premises of libraries for
those books embrittled in storage.

Deacidification is probably the most important process
in the preservation of paper, but it must be understood what
this neutralization of acid will and will not do.   It does not
decrease the probability of biological attacks, because some
fungi thrive in alkaline conditions.   Nor does deacidification
prevent oxidative decay or photochemical reaction, although
alkaline buffering agents will neutralize any acid by-products
of such attacks.   Deacidification will not strengthen paper
already embrittled by acid hydrolysis.   On the other hand,
deacidification does arrest the deterioration and embrittlement of paper by introducing a strong base (a chemical term
for an alkaline material) to form neutral salts with the sul-
furic acid.   The excess neutralizer, however, must also be
easily convertible to neutral salts so that the paper will not
be subject to subsequent alkaline hydrolysis.   These same
neutral salts should act as buffering agents to prevent future
acid contamination from any source.

It is important from the point of view of practicality
that deacidification treatments be inexpensive, simple to perform, suitable for mechanization, and above all, have no
adverse effects on books, paper, or people.

The marketing in the 1970s of a nonaqueous deacidification solution that can be sprayed on acid book paper from aerosol cans or from spray bottles has made a major impact on library conservation programs. No longer is it necessary to disassemble and later rebind valuable and often irreplaceable books in research libraries and rare book rooms of public and university libraries to deacidify acid book pages that would ultimately self-destruct if not so treated. This has reduced the cost for deacidification of single volumes from hundreds of dollars to something in the order of ten to twenty dollars per book, depending on size. This was a great stride forward and will be a mainstay in library conservation until some of the mass deacidification techniques under development at the Public Archives of Canada and the Library of Congress[13] are released for general use.

Nonaqueous deacidification is described in detail in the Library of Congress Publication on Conservation, Series #500 No. 2.[14] Dr. Smith's instructions for nonaqueous deacidification[15] using commercially available Wei T'o are considerably easier to read and follow.

Aqueous deacidification techniques are described in equal detail in the Library of Congress Publication on Conservation, Series 500 No. 1[16] and the National Archives Publication on Conservation Technology, 1979.[17] Much simpler instructions using a solution made with milk of magnesia and club soda is available in the Abbey Newsletter of July 1978. The Library of Congress publication[16] also includes simple instructions for making a deacidifier in a seltzer bottle. It is reproduced in Appendix I.

Regardless of the system used, the acid in paper should never be neutralized until the ink on the paper has first been tested for solubility in the deacidifier liquid. When ink on printed or written materials is soluble in both aqueous and nonaqueous deacidifier solvents, thus precluding their use, mildly acid paper can be neutralized by the vapor phase deacidification technique.[18] Chemically impregnated VPD sheets are available from the North American distributors[19] of the British product.

Mending and Reinforcing Paper

The traditional techniques for mending paper with handmade paper and vegetable paste are best learned by working under

the instruction of those who have become expert by long
practice.   It is not easy and requires much practice on expendable materials before repair on materials in the collections should be attempted.   For those who wish to try and
cannot get on-hands instruction from an expert, we recommend practice following the instructions prepared at the
Northeast Document Conservation Center (Appendix E).   Other good guidances have been written by Melvyn Jones[20] and
Paul Mucci. [21]

Mending Tape

English manufacturers in collaboration with conservation
specialists in that country have developed a "pressure sensitive archival quality mending tape"[22] that the distributors
claim does not adversely affect paper as do the commercial
tapes so often used in the past for paper repair.   Our tests
reveal that when artificially aged for the equivalent of twenty-
eight years of natural aging, this product retains its adhesion and does not stain or discolor paper.   We consider it
suitable for mending of tears in circulating library materials, reference volumes in undergraduate libraries, and
repair of tears in documents that are important only for the
information on them.   We cannot suggest that this archival
repair tape be used on volumes in rare book rooms, documentary materials that are important as objects as well as
for their information, prints and drawings, maps, broadsides, etc.

Heat-Set Mending Tissue

A thermoplastic mending tissue developed at the Library of
Congress[23] can be used for quick and easy repairs of torn
paper using a tacking iron or household flatiron for application.   This, too, tests well under artificial aging, but
again, we recommend it only for use on book pages and
documentary materials that have no special value as objects.
Because this is awkward to make according to the Library
of Congress's instructions, we recommend that it be obtained from August Velletri, Bookmakers, 2025 Eye Street,
N. W. , Washington, D. C. if you wish to experiment with the
material.

Polyester Film Encapsulation

Encapsulation of brittle or heavily worn documents, prints and drawings, broadsides and maps has proven to be a boon to librarians and archivists since it was developed at the Library of Congress about ten years ago. [24] This technique for reinforcing damaged paper is simple, inexpensive, requires no investment in capital equipment and can be mastered by a novice in a very brief time. In some establishments it has supplanted the lamination of paper with cellulose acetate applied by heat and pressure which for a long time has been regarded by some as the ultimate in protection for heavily used materials. There are literally dozens of good printed instructions from commercial sources and preservation laboratories, including the one in Appendix E in this book. The Library of Congress instruction[24] is more complete. Those who have a requirement for encapsulating large numbers of documents might wish to consider a machine for this purpose. [25] They are expensive, but save time and the results are uniformly excellent.

Reinforcing with Nylon Webb

Polyester film encapsulation is generally too bulky for reinforcing book paper, although some heavily used atlases and similar material can be post-bound after the individual plates have been encapsulated. If, for any reason, it is necessary to salvage and rebind the brittle pages of a book, that can be done by applying nylon gossamer webb to each page (after the book has been disassembled and the pages deacidified and buffered) as described in Appendix E. This reinforcement is strong and barely noticeable and after application, the pages can then be assembled into gatherings, sewn on cords or tapes, fastened to boards, etc. by the conventional binding process in a hand bindery or by a library binding establishment.

Book Cover Repairs

By far the best instructions available for simple repairs to cased book covers are those in Carolyn Horton's 1969 Cleaning and Preserving Bindings and Related Materials [3238], which is still obtainable from the American Library Association's Library Technology Project.

Portfolios and Boxes

When single documents, thin pamphlets and similar materials require more physical protection than encapsulation or
file folders, they can be put in an easily made protective
wrapper.   Instructions for a particularly good design, because it can be cut to fit anything from single sheets to
pamphlets or even thin books, is Willman Spawn's, reproduced with his permission in Appendix F1+2.   Another easily made wrapper is the one designed at Brown University
Library, Appendix F3.

Not too long ago before the inflation of the fifties,
sixties, and seventies, it was possible to buy at a modest
cost sturdy protective boxes for rare books, beautifully
made with full leather covers or with leather spines and
marbled paper sides and all fully lined with soft materials.
Other equally handsome and sturdy solander or clam shell
type boxes, cloth covered and labeled to resemble books
were available in the 1960s for as little as ten dollars each
for smaller books.   Today the cost of similar items is warranted only for the most precious materials in a rare book
room.

Thirty years later the requirement for protective
covers for dilapidated books being greater than ever, librarians are resorting to aesthetically less pleasing, but
affordable protective covers.   The phase boxes designed
over a period of years at the Library of Congress[26] have
been frequently copied in books and pamphlets on book care.
We believe that in addition to Willman Spawn's pattern for
smaller and thinner volumes, the inexpensive protective
boxes made at the Northeast Document Conservation Center
(Appendix F4) patterned after the Library of Congress' basic
designs can be made in any library in-house workshop to
meet the great majority of the requirements of that library.

Prints and Drawings

Those working in in-house workshops in libraries, archives,
and historical societies should be most conservative in regard to the treatment of prints, drawings, and photographs.
Colored works of art on paper requiring treatment should
always be sent to professional conservators.   Nonprofes-
sionals should strictly limit themselves to dry (surface) cleaning of black and white prints and pictures and photographs

and replacing acid carboard or wood supports for framed
materials with museum quality mounting board backings.
An eloquent warning of the problems in cleaning drawings
was provided in 1975 by Roy Graf. [27] Excellent instructions
in technique for cleaning prints and drawings are available
in slide form from the Smithsonian Institution. [4]

The special problem of treatment for architectural
drawings is being studied in depth by the Committee for the
Preservation of Architectural Records (COPAR).   Reports
of their activities are published quarterly in a news letter
from the Library of Congress. [28]   Practical suggestions for
treating these often embrittled materials were published in
Technology and Conservation in 1976. [29]

Conservation Workshop Equipment

When funds are available a workshop for a large establishment should include:

1. A 30" x 72" fume hood over a 30" x 48" sink*
2. A 30" x 72" workbench with a 24" x 24" light box
    in the top and shelving and drawers for storage
    below*
3. A 36" x 48" x 76" (high) silk screen drying rack
4. High intensity light
5. Hand held magnifier
6. Hand held ultraviolet illuminator
7. Hand held motor driven spray equipment
8. Dry mounting press (20" x 24")
9. One letter press (12" x 15" plates)
10. Assorted cleaning materials: knives, brushes,
    straight edges, rules, squares
11. Six plastic photographer's trays of assorted sizes
12. A 22" x 36" x 48" thymol cabinet (see page 108
    Conservation of Library Materials [7261]**

*These items can be manufactured by a local carpenter,
metalsmith and plumber.   Costs will depend on local
labor and material costs.

**As an alternative to a thymol chamber built on the
premises by local labor one can consider the 30 cubic
foot vacuum fumigator manufactured and sold by Vacudyne Corp. , Chicago, ILL.

Smaller repositories in which it is planned to do some in-house treatment should have:

1. A Barrow Test Kit, available from: Applied Sciences Laboratories, Inc. , 2216 Hull St. , Richmond, VA 23224
2. pH Indicator test strips*
3. Spray deacidifier. Wei T'o Associates, Inc. , 224 Early Street, P. O. Box 332, Park Forest, Illinois 60406
4. Polyester film for encapsulation*
5. Double Faced Tape for encapsulation*
6. Nylon gossamer web for reinforcing. Process Materials, 301 Veterans Blvd. , Rutherford, NJ 07070
7. Thermoplastic nylon for use with the nylon gossamer web. TALAS, 130 5th Ave. , New York, NY
8. A supply of white blotters (30" x 40" or larger)*
9. An assortment of erasers and architect's cleaning pads from a local supplier*
10. Silicone Release Paper for use in nylon web reinforcement. TALAS, 130 5th Ave. , New York, NY
11. A supply of handmade European paper for book repair*
12. A small supply of various Japanese mulberry papers for document repair*
13. A supply of several thicknesses of good quality museum board, card stock, etc. for portfolio and box making*

*Available from most supply houses

Leaf Cast Paper Repairs for Documents

It is now possible to fill holes in paper documents, replace missing corners, and build up eroded edges by the leaf casting technique[30] in a small workshop, if it has a 30" x 48" x 6" sink. Hand-held sheet formers for this purpose costing only one-twentieth the cost of the mechanized devices used at the Library of Congress and the Northeast Document Conservation Center are available with complete instructions for their use from the New Jersey manufacturer.[31] These are recommended for use by in-house workshop staffs in those establishments that have established long-range programs for large quantities of record materials.

In Conclusion

In-house conservation is a controversial subject and some
suggestions presented in this chapter for your consideration
are not universally accepted.   There is general agreement
on the overriding need for preventive conservation such as
climate control and control of light, better storage and handling, better material control, and for widespread training
and education of librarians and archivists in conservation
management.   However, there is little agreement on what
librarians and archivists can do in-house with their own
staff, student help, or volunteers.   Several years ago we
expressed our views on this matter, [32] stressing the fact
that general acceptance of "in-house" treatments is vitally
important if we are ever going to make any progress in
saving the millions of books that are already unsafe to use
or are rapidly becoming so.   Two days later at the same
conference the director of a very distinguished library in
the Central States took issue with our position[33] and expressed the fear that "in-house" restoration might turn out
to be more like "outhouse" restoration.   Such a shocking
statement would normally not deserve the dignity of a re-
buttal, but because of it, we can only conclude that some
people regard librarians as incapable of decision-making,
self-discipline and, in general, managing their own affairs.
We take the opposite view, and the recommendations in this
book are based on our premise that the library profession
must take charge.

References

1. See Appendices E and F for NEDCC's recommended
      procedures for cleaning, mending and reinforcing pa-
      per and boxmaking.

2. See Appendix F for Library of Congress instructions.

3. Yale University Library Preservation Pamphlets on
      Wraparounds (No. 1), Tip-ins and Pockets (No. 2),
      Paper Treatment (No. 3), Pamphlet Binding (No. 4),
      The Small Bindery (No. 5).   Available from Yale
      University Library, New Haven, Connecticut 06520.

4. The Cleaning of Prints, Drawings and Manuscripts: Dry
      Methods (3-4).   Washington: Smithsonian Institution,
      Office of Museum Programs, 1977.   A 35-mm slide/

audio cassette combination.   The Removal of Pressure Sensitive Tape from Flat Paper (V81).   Washington: Smithsonian Institution, Office of Management Programs (n. d.).   A twenty minute video tape instruction.

5.   Fortson-Jones, Judith (ed.).   Surface Cleaning.   Lincoln: Nebraska State Historical Society, 1980.   A set of 82 35-mm slides intended for audiences with little or no experience.

6.   Basic Preservation Procedures Kit 70.   Washington: Association of Research Libraries, Office of Management Studies, 1981.

7.   Berger, Pearl.   "Minor Repairs in a Small Research Library," Library Journal 104(12):1311-1317, 1979.

8.   Northeast Document Conservation Center, Abbot Hall, School St. , Andover, MA 01810.

9.   Guild of Book Workers, 663 Fifth Avenue, New York, New York 10022.

10.   Society of American Archivists, 330 S. Wells St. (Suite 810), Chicago, Illinois 60606.

11.   American Institute for Conservation, 1511 K Street, N. W. , Washington, D. C. 20005.

12.   Hofenk-de Graaff, J. "The Cleaning of Paper," Yearbook of Paper History 1980.   Basle: International Association of Paper Historians, 1980.

13.   See Chapter V.

14.   Deacidification--Magnesium Methyl Carbonate Non-Aqueous Treatment.   Washington: Library of Congress (working draft July 1977).

15.   Smith, Richard D.   "Paper Deacidification," Art Dealer and Framer November 1976 and December 1976.

_____.   "The Deacidification of Paper and Books," American Libraries 6(2):108-110, 1975.

16. The Deacidification and Alkalization of Documents with
     Magnesium Bicarbonate. Washington: Library of
     Congress (working draft 1978).

17. Wilson, W. K. (et al.). Preparation of Solutions of
     Magnesium Bicarbonate for Deacidification of Docu-
     ments. Washington: National Archives, 1979.

18. Ede, J. R. and W. H. Langwell. "Sulphur Dioxide and
     Vapour Phase Deacidification," Proceedings of the
     Conference of the International Institute for Conser-
     vation 1968. London: IIC, 1969.

19. The Campbell-Logan Bindery (Interleaf). 212 Second
     St. North, Minneapolis, MN 55401.

20. Jones, Melvyn. "Traditional Repair of Archival Docu-
     ments," The Paper Conservator 3:9-17, 1978.

21. Mucci, Paul. "Technical Notes--Mending Book and
     Document Papers with Long Fibered Japanese Tis-
     sues," Mid-Atlantic Archivist 5(2):5-16, 1976.

22. Archival Aids, Division of Ademco Limited, Ademco
     Photo/Graphic, Ltd., 1000 Jay St., P.O. Box
     111A, Rochester, N.Y. 14601.

23. Heat-Set Tissue Preparation and Application. Library
     of Congress, Conservation Workshop Notes Series
     300 No. 1, Working draft August 1976.

24. Polyester Film Encapsulation. Washington: The Li-
     brary of Congress, 1980.

25. The Young "Radiowelder" is available from The Hol-
     linger Corporation, Post Office Box 6185, Arlington,
     Virginia 22206. Another model incorporating "ultra-
     sonic welding" for sealing the film is available from
     William Minter & Peter Malosh, 1948 West Addison
     St., Chicago, Illinois 60613.

26. Brown, Margaret. Boxes for the Protection of Rare
     Books: Their Design and Construction. Washing-
     ton: The Library of Congress, 1982.

27. "Problems in Connection with the Cleaning of Drawings,"
     Canadian Conservation Institute Newsletter 6:3-5,
     1975.

28. A Newsletter for COPAR.   Washington: Library of
     Congress, Central Service Division, Printing and
     Processing Section (a quarterly).

29. Seamans, W. A.   "Restoring Architectural Drawings:
     An Economical Method for Treating Embrittled
     Documents," Technology and Conservation Winter
     1976, pp. 8-11.

30. Blun, Denis and Guy Petherbridge.   "Leaf casting--the
     mechanical repair of paper artifacts," The Paper
     Conservator 1:26-32, 1976.

31. Union Instrument Company, Inc. , 1447 East 2nd Street,
     Plainfield, New Jersey 07061.

32. At the June 1974 Pre Conference Meeting of the Rare
     Books and Manuscripts Section of the Association
     of College and Research Libraries.

33. See A. B. Bookman's Weekly 54(5):462, 1974.

Chapter IX

THE 1980s AND BEYOND

It is unlikely that the library as a storehouse of books
will be replaced by a computer in the basement with
remote consoles.   The bulk of a student's inquiries,
even thirty years from now, will be with books and
other tangible materials stored within the local library.   If anything, the use of technology will require more space for equipment and create pressures
for more user-space than the book-oriented one.

> --The Impact of Technology
> on the Library Building.
> New York, N.Y.:   Edu-
> cational and Facilities
> Laboratories, Inc., 1967,
> p. 11.

Twenty-five years ago, well before the new technology began
making significant changes in the ways information is stored
for rapid retrieval, it was predicted that these new developments would compound conservation problems.   From the
point of view of preservation that is becoming a reality.   It
is not appropriate for conservators to inject themselves into
the management problems in regard to the use of electronic
publishing versus the traditional book forms, micropublishing,
and other exotic data storage and recovery systems.   We
(the authors of this book) know that the new technologies are
here to stay and being bibliophiles and bibliomaniacs are following these new developments with more than professional
interest.   F.W. Lancaster, probably the foremost advocate
of the hypothesis that "the library of the future will be a
home or office television set"[1] argues his beliefs with conviction.[2]   Certainly no one can dispute his reasoning insofar
as it pertains to the publication of technical and scientific

journals and regularly revised and updated general reference
material, particularly for special libraries in the professional and business world.   There are equally cogent arguments
that the printed book will be around for a long time to come.
Those who support this position accept the premise that "the
revolution in the transmission of knowledge will certainly
solve many current problems."[3]   They also contend that
"books will continue to exist because there will always be a
need for them to exist."[4]   Also, they remind us that "real
books have functions beyond the conveyance of information,
just as the human mind is much more than an organ for the
storage of facts.   "Books have the qualities of the minds that
produce them."[5]

Vast quantities of printed books now in library stacks
(and a significant proportion of those that will continue to be
printed) will have to be preserved.   Most librarians on both
sides agree that "the new means of storing information are
unlikely (from the very dim vantage point of today) to retro-
spectively convert all existing printed matter into the new
electronic formats."[6] From now on librarians will have the
added responsibility of preserving a prodigious amount of
electronically processed information, as well as audio and
video tapes, optical discs, and microforms so rapidly accumulating.   All of these forms being man-made out of man-
made materials are far from being indestructable.   In some
instances they will be more vulnerable to heat, humidity,
water damage, atmospheric pollution, and electro-magnetic
radiation than other library collections.   The amounts of
money now being spent annually in commercial and academic
computer facilities to stabilize the climate and filter dust,
dirt, and noxious chemicals from circulating air are not
modest.   Hard-pressed librarians in the same establishments
who have been trying unsuccessfully for years for the same
climate control in their storage areas must often inwardly
rage.

As so well documented[7] preservation is no longer the
province of the few.   Today librarians, archivists, conservators, conservation scientists, hand bookbinders, commercial binders, publishers, papermakers, and the professional
societies are now in general agreement that the heretofore
alarming deterioration of books and records can be controlled
and are collaborating more and more to that end.   The motivation has been mostly altruistic but the aims of some
(happily only a few) have been unmistakably self-serving,
camouflaged by pretensions of concern for the preservation

of the integrity of objects.   An extreme example of that is
the recent proposal for copyrighting art restorations (which
could include rare books and other records) to give conservators "control of their storage, display and further work
on their restoration after they have been returned to their
owners."[8]

It is fully expected that librarians and archivists in
the 1980s and beyond will embrace conservation as a cost-
effective management tool to reduce loss by decay, fire,
theft, vandalism, natural disasters, and normal wear and
tear to help meet their ever increasing responsibilities with
ever decreasing financial support.   Most repositories, some
begrudgingly, will have a conservation program of some
sort.   Because no two are alike there will be a great variety of programs to meet the varying requirements, depending on the size of collections, resources, and user requirements.   For some, simple prevention (climate control, control of light, better housekeeping and storage, etc.) will
suffice in order to extend the useful life of ultimately expendable materials.   At the other extreme, major research
libraries with large and varied collections will have more
comprehensive programs of preventive and restorative measures making maximum use of in-house and professional resources.

In 1981 Ellen McCrady made a rather thorough analysis of priorities for conservation advocated by various
agencies and professional groups during the preceding five
years.[9]   As she observed, each advocated program has much
merit but each differs from the rest in the importance it
assigns to the elements in each program.   There never will
be agreement nor is there need for agreement.   Each library
and archive must establish its own priorities according to the
requirements of those who use it and the conditions that prevail in that geographic area and that particular building.   In
our opinion, these are the general considerations that must
be looked into in organizing any conservation program--the
listed order is not necessarily an order of priorities: security, disaster and disaster planning, environment control,
housing and storage, organizing for conservation, education
and training, cooperative conservation, local and regional
programs, commercial binding control, in-house care of
materials, use of professional services, brittle book programs, care of non-print materials, treatment of collections
as a whole rather than treatment of objects, phased conservation programs, periodic surveys and frequent reviews of
progress.

In regard to overall conservation requirements during
the next two decades, it is our opinion that emphasis should
be in these areas: training at the graduate level of conservators and conservation administrators, more continuing
education opportunities in conservation-oriented subjects at
colleges and universities, more emphasis on conservation
in degree requirements at colleges of library and information science, development of standards for treatment of various categories of books and other materials, development of
good quality paper for books of permanent value, improved
materials and processing procedures for preservation microfilming, expansion of basic research in conservation areas,
more regional conservation centers, and state and regional
clearinghouses for conservation information.

The assertion, all too frequently heard from within
the ranks of professional conservation, that a "dearth of information for conservation guidance is prejudicial to the development of library conservation" just cannot be sustained.
The more than five thousand citations in the general bibliography to this book, in addition to the almost five thousand
listed in our previous book Conservation of Library Materials [7261], plus the many references at the end of each
chapter of this volume deny that specious claim of obviously
self-interested individuals.

Interest in planning for conservation of library and
archival materials has been heavily weighted towards the
needs of paper records, especially bound volumes.   That
does not mean, however, that the preservation needs of all
other library materials have been dangerously neglected as
claimed by Pamela Darling. 10 The one area that perhaps
has been neglected is that of the care of motion picture and
TV film and tapes.   A grim report of the magnitude of that
problem in England (undoubtedly the same in the U.S.) is in
the June 1981 Journal of the Royal Society of Art. 11 This
suggests what librarians and others can expect in the next
twenty years as the non-paper materials increase in their
collections with the accelerated developments in the new
technology.   This is only the latest proof of the age-old
fact that there is always a tremendous gap between our ability to make things and our ability to care for them.   It is
the time now for librarians and archivists through their professional associations to underwrite studies on the care of
these new materials so that they will not be overwhelmed in
the early 21st century by problems in connection with conservation that will dwarf the conservation problems librarians
have had to contend with in the last twenty years.

Regardless of the revolution in the transmission and storage of information using the new technologies, librarians are naïve if they think that there will be a corresponding reduction in preservation requirements (and cost) as the use of non-book materials proliferates.   There can never be innovation without collateral problems.   When information is gathered and stored in any manner it is only the beginning and not the ending of its career.   It is normal for material things regardless of the substance to deteriorate with age.

What we have stressed in this book is that when custodians began to take charge of this vital aspect of their everyday work their attitudes in regard to conservation began to change from gloom and despair to a more positive attitude that something could be done to save our books and other records.   One must acknowledge the many important contributions by professional conservators and the scientific community which will continue, but progress in conservation to-date and the momentum now associated with it has been mainly the result of competent and forceful leadership from within the library and archives professions.   Conservation leadership will remain in the library community.   We are pleased to note that our position is supported by the Delphi study completed in 1981 by Donald Bruce McKeon as part of his doctoral dissertation at the University of Florida (see summary in Appendix N).   The purpose of the Delphi study according to McKeon was:

1. to establish the probable lines of development of both the conservation of materials in libraries and archives and of training for this field in the period 1981-2001;
2. to detect any significant differences between the futures envisioned by two groups involved with the problem;
3. to determine the degree of firmness of opinion of persons concerned with the field.

Two respondent groups [25 professional library educators nominated by their schools and 19 individuals presently active in the conservation field at regional and national levels (preservationists)] were supplied a free-answer preliminary questionnaire (Round One).   Answers to this questionnaire provided the definitive test instrument (Rounds Two and Three).

Each group of respondents was returned this test instrument with the group means included after Round Two and offered the opportunity to change their responses.   Only 2. 4 percent of responses were altered when the means of the groups were presented (elimination of one respondent would have given a change rate of 1. 7 percent), indicating a high degree of individualism and lack of concern for a group consensus.

The future as predicted by the study will involve economic stringency, shortage of trained personnel, and some governmental conservation responsibilities.

Materials in greatest danger (post-1980) will be treated at outside centers, with heavy use of microfilming.   Respondents were undecided as to technology.   Custodians will select materials to preserve and conservation administrators will be trained for wide knowledge rather than bench experience.   Library schools will want trained conservators for instruction and some test or degree mechanism from an existing installation will constitute professional entrance.

Statistical analysis using the non-parametric Mann-Whitney test indicated that the populations of educators and preservationists do not differ significantly in the developments predicted for the conservation field.   The Delphi study technique is extensively used for future predictions and experience indicated that with expert groups exceeding fifteen respondents predictions have a high degree of reliability. This study employed a total of 44 respondents as statistical analysis indicated that the two groups could be legitimately merged.

The following poignant comment by McKeon after the conclusion of his study is only one more reason why the keepers of the records of our heritage must take charge of their conservation:

One of the most interesting and perhaps significant results of the study is the confirmation of what many of us have experimentally noted: those in the conservation field hold their views very strongly and have little concern about whether their views are commonly-held or not. [12]

Because of the major changes in government since 1980 with drastic cuts in federal, state, and local support and correspondingly greater demands on private agencies, librarians and archivists will have to do more with less as time goes on.   Reduced funding means that things which only

a few years ago might have seemed trivial are now of much
importance and matters which have always been important
are now doubly so.   Librarians who always have been concerned about book deterioration will now have to be even
more conscientious.   Managers who before have taken spo-
radic flings at conservation will have to establish conservation programs in self-defense.   Those who have been over-
whelmingly service oriented will have to be able to embrace
conservation in order to be able to continue their services
to the academic community and the general reading public.
In libraries that are predominantly service oriented "librarians will have to do some soul-searching and reconsider
their priorities and services and decide to keep all of them
at the expense of preventive conservation or sacrifice a
cherished but not necessarily vital program in order to keep
the books that are the reason for a librarian's existence in
usable condition."[13]

Robert Patterson, editor of Conservation Administration News and Director of Libraries at the University of
Tulsa wisely observes:

We would argue that preservation is not the concern of a
small elite group (if indeed it ever was).   It is an effort
to preserve our national documentary heritage.
Preservation will not wither on the vine without grant
support.   The seeds of the 70s are too well planted, but
it now becomes much more our individual responsibilities
to see that the effort is carried forward.   Local initia-
tives and resourcefulness should see the creation of new
programs in the 80s, which will strengthen the grass
roots network, created by the grants of the 70s.   It will
certainly be harder work without the largesse of federal
assistance, but I think we will be surprised to find the
number of options available to us, using locally generated
resources.[14]

Robert Patterson, deeply involved in conservation (as
are other professional librarians and archivists) is an excellent example of the capable, well-informed leadership in library ranks that is pioneering this important aspect of library science.   His recommendations for organizing for conservation in the Library Journal's special series on preservation in 1979,[15] amplified and expanded in his address at
the 1981 Allerton Park Institute,[6] should be regarded as conservation doctrine for libraries.   We are in complete agreement with his thesis that conservation as a management func-

tion will be the greatest challenge to the library profession
in the next twenty years.   The following is a summary of
his and our views on conservation management which are
parallel.

In the serious economic situation of the 1980s, the
major support libraries have enoyed is diminishing. At the
same time great advantages and opportunities are taking place
in preservation. Conservation must be put in a broad perspective.   Now when resources are smaller, and with all the
existing programs libraries are struggling to provide, librarians must add another expensive program--conservation.
In order to meet their professional responsibilities librarians
must develop preservation programs and at the same time
develop stronger critical ability about what to save and how
to go about it.   And librarians as overall managers must be
the ones to develop these programs.

Librarians must take the responsibility for educating
themselves about conservation to the point where they can
design and implement their own programs.   "To wait for the
conservator in most libraries is like waiting for Godot" because there are just not enough conservators; and at this
time, although there are some promising developments, conservation does not generally have an accepted curriculum.
Librarians will take control of conservation in their establishments as they have learned to use another technology--
that of automation.   Preservation will be considered as a
part of collection development, for only librarians, in close
consort with the academic community, can make the management decisions in regard to what must be preserved in its
original form and what must be kept available, (frequently
in another format) for its intellectual content only.

Conservation will continue to be expensive and conservation decisions will continue to demand the greatest of
critical judgment weighing all of the aspects of library science against the preservation considerations.   There will be
a steady increase in cooperative efforts in conservation from
the simplest levels of information sharing to the establishment of sophisticated regional centers and other conservation
consortiums as a means of reducing management costs, increasing management competence, and efficient disaster reaction capability.   Preservation management programs, depending on the size of the institutions will be along these
lines:

a) an understanding of the factors affecting the physical environment and what is necessary to control them.
b) comprehensive disaster prevention and recovery plans.
c) positive control of binding preparation and binding practices.
d) frequent recourse to professional conservation expertise and facilities.
e) an in-house capability for preventive conservation and simple repair.
f) emphasis on treatment of collections as a whole rather than the treatment of single items.
g) in-house conservation training and indoctrination for staff.
h) education of users in conservation and the need for their collaboration.
i) participation in cooperative conservation efforts at all levels.
j) concentration on alternative sources for funding from the local to the national level.

In Conclusion

Conservation, already a matter of national concern, is the greatest challenge the library and archival professions will face in the next two decades as the present well-known problems are exacerbated by new issues related to the new technologies. There is ample evidence from what has been accomplished to date by some innovators in libraries and archives throughout the length and breadth of this land that the two professions are more than equal to the confrontation. It now remains for others in these vocations to carry on BECAUSE CONSERVATION IS MANAGEMENT.

References

1. Kleiman, Dena. "Or a trip to the library by computer," Boston Herald American March 31, 1980.

2. Lancaster, F. Wilfred. "The Future of the Librarian Lies Outside the Library," Catholic Library World 51(9):388-391, 1980.

_____. "The Research Library of 2001," Oklahoma Librarian 30(4):42-47, 1980.

_____. "Mission possible--a future information system," Canadian Library Journal 36(6):339-342, 1979.

3.   Piternick, Anne B.   "The challenge to bibliographic
      control," Canadian Library Journal 36(6):343-346,
      1979.

4.   Baker, J. William.   "Will public libraries be obsolete
      in the 1980s?" Canadian Library Journal 36(5):262-
      268, 1979.

5.   Bailey, Herbert S.   "The Traditional Book in the Elec-
      tronic Age: A Compelling Evaluation of a Modern
      Day Issue," Publishers Weekly December 5, 1977.
      Reprinted in Library Scene 7(2):24-30, 1978.

6.   Patterson, R. H.   "Conservation: What Should We Do
      Until the Conservator and the Twenty-First Century
      Arrive?" Keynote Address at the Twenty-Seventh
      Allerton Park Institute, University of Illinois at
      Urbana-Champaign, November 1981.

7.   Darling, P. W. and Sherelyn Ogden.   "From Problems
      Perceived to Programs in Practice: The Preserva-
      tion of Library Resources in the U. S. A. 1956-80,"
      Library Resources and Technical Services 25:9-29,
      Jan. 1981.

8.   "For Activist Conservators: Copyright," The Abbey
      Newsletter 5(5):59, 1981.   The editor ANL com-
      ments on an article "Copyright Art Restorations" in
      the April 1981 Bulletin of the Copyright Society USA.

9.   McCrady, Ellen.   "Priorities in Library and Archival
      Conservation," The Abbey Newsletter 5(2):17-20,
      1981.

      _____.   "Priorities in Library and Archival Conser-
      vation II," The Abbey Newsletter 5(6):67-70, 1981.

10.   Darling, P. W.   "Creativity vs. Despair" Library
      Trends 30(2):179-188, Fall 1981.

11.   Royal Society of Arts Journal 129(5299):423-434, 1981.

12.   Personal letter D. B. McKeon to G. M. Cunha dated
      November 11, 1981.

13.   Riechel, Rosemarie.   "Public Libraries: A Method of
      Survival Through Prevention," Catholic Library
      World 51(4):162-165, 1979.

14.   Patterson, R. H.   "An Accolade to the NEH and
        NHPRC and a Guardedly Hopeful Comment on the
        Future," Conservation Administration News Number
        7, June 1981 (page 2).

15.   _____. "Organizing for Conservation," Library
        Journal 109:1116-1119, 1979.

Appendix A

PRINCIPLES OF CONSERVATION AND RESTAURATION IN LIBRARIES

The text of these Principles has been compiled and agreed by the members of the Standing Committee of the IFLA Section on Conservation. It is published in the IFLA Journal in this form as a means of presenting the text to the widest Library community.

It is intended that translations of the text in French, German and Russian should appear in relevant library journals.

The purpose of these Principles is to establish a responsible attitude to conservation and restoration in libraries and to encourage those entrusted with the care of library and archive collections, old and new, to formulate a positive policy on the future of these collections.

The Standing Committee invites comments upon these Principles and these should be sent to the Secretary of the IFLA Section on Conservation, Mr. Peter Brown, Librarian of Trinity College, College Street, Dublin 2, Ireland.

Preamble

The aim and purpose of a library is preservation in its widest sense: to collect the documents (manuscript, printed and in other forms) of the past and of the present, and to keep them so that they are available to both present and future users.

It is extremely difficult to formulate principles that can provide guidance on the collection of the significant documents of the past and of the present in this and future centuries. This difficulty is clearly reflected by the deficiencies in library collections of some categories of document which, although perhaps intended as of solely local and ephemeral interest, can form a part of the evidence for the history of civilisations.

It is also not a simple matter to formulate in general terms those preventative and curative measures that will ensure that the existing and known cultural patrimony in libraries can survive far into the future. It is with these measures of conservation and restoration that the following principles are concerned.

In order that he may fully understand conservation and restoration problems a librarian responsible for this very special task must gain some knowledge and feeling not only for the scientific basis, the techniques and materials of conservation and restoration measures, but also for the origin and history of the items in his collections, by their physical composition as well as by their contents.

It is essential that both librarians and restorers should recognize that they have to deal with objects of various kinds and of various natures that have arisen from various historical cultures, traditions and technologies. As far as possible restoration treatment on each object should be carried out in a way that is sympathetic to its origins.

1.   Nature and objectives of these Principles

1.1   This statement of Principles represents a general approach towards the nature and objectives of conservation and restoration work for library collections.   It does not therefore aim to provide a comprehensive picture of detailed methods and practices, but is intended to establish a responsible attitude to conservation and restoration in libraries.

1.2   The technical means by which the objectives of conservation and restoration may be best achieved in a given case must always be decided upon jointly by librarians and by technical and scientific conservation and restoration experts.   The choice of materials for conservation and restoration treatment needs to be based on highly expert assessment by scientific experts.   The treatment must be performed by or under the control of fully trained technical experts.

1.3   The dangers to their collections are known but librarians and curators frequently do not proclaim sufficiently loudly the consequences of neglect. The purpose of this statement of principles is to encourage those responsible for the care of collections to face up to these consequences and, together with their technical and scientific experts, to formulate a positive policy on the future of their collections.

1.4   By this means national and even international policies on the preservation of library materials can be established.   It is necessary to emphasize that such policies have to be applied equally to the library materials produced in the present as well as to those produced in the past.

2.   General observations on Conservation

2.1   The materials of collections in libraries consist primarily in organic matter and are therefore inherently perishable.   The process of decay can, however, be slowed down considerably by creating favourable storage conditions.

2.2   The precautions to be taken in the interests of the conservation of library material are fundamentally to provide a suitable environment for it. This means that the following areas of responsibility must receive attention:
a)   controlled climatic environment
b)   level of lighting
c)   cleanliness of storage areas
d)   suitability of storage materials
e)   precautions against physical damage, particularly in the handling of library materials.

2.3   The climatic factors of temperature and humidity, light and airborne contaminants (including dust) all cause degradation reactions.   The chemical nature of these reactions may vary for different materials, but the following general principles apply.

2. 4   There is a close relationship between temperature and relative humidity and it must be remembered that temperature changes cause variations in humidity.   Temperature and humidity should therefore both be at a satisfactory level in library storage and reading room areas.   The climatic conditions in these areas should be monitored adequately with reliable and regularly checked recording apparatus.   A word of warning to librarians is needed on the dangers of a possible sudden change of climatic conditions when library collections are moved from uncontrolled conditions into areas with mechanical air control systems.

2. 5   Coolness is preferable to a high temperature.   For the conservation of books and manuscripts a constant temperature of not more than 18° C is recommended.   A lower temperature is acceptable (even preferable) as long as it is accompanied by humidity control.   At higher temperatures the possibility of damage increases and 25° C is a point at which dangerous conditions arise.   For some special materials (e. g. film) there are specific temperature requirements that demand much lower temperatures.

2. 6   The relative humidity (RH) and consequently the equilibrium moisture content (EMC) of organic library material must be maintained at a constant level.   A stable relative humidity of 50%-55% is recommended.   A higher relative humidity leads to increased biological change; on the other hand a lower relative humidity can be harmful, since organic material needs to retain sufficient moisture to remain flexible.   Significant fluctuations in humidity lead to changes in the volume of the various organic substances of which library materials consist, and can introduce conditions of stress that produce cracks, distortion or other damage.   There are specific humidity requirements for some special materials (e. g. film).

2. 7   Light in all forms promotes the decay of organic materials; ultraviolet light is the most dangerous.   Light levels must therefore be kept as low as possible, both in storage and in use conditions.   Storage conditions should ideally be dark, but if in natural light all windows should be overlaid with UV filters and provision should be made (e. g. with blinds) to reduce any heat gain.   It may be necessary to provide UV filters for artificial lighting. In reading rooms the light level falling on library materials should not be more than 100 lux (and preferably UV filtered).   In exhibition cases the constant level falling on the surface of library materials should not be more than 50 lux and all lighting must be UV filtered.   Lighting level and the UV content of light should be measured (standard photometer and UV monitor) in all areas containing library materials.

2. 8   New library buildings should be designed to meet as far as possible conservation requirements.   This will affect many aspects: design and orientation of buildings, building materials (which can under some circumstances be used to produce satisfactory internal, climatic conditions in preference to mechanical air control systems), internal building and furnishing materials and materials used for furniture including shelving, lighting both natural and artificial.

2. 9   Airborne contaminants are a source of damage to library collections especially to leather and to ground wood paper.   In areas of heavy pollution it may be necessary to protect library collections by air purification.

2. 10   It may be regarded as unrealistic to aim at the best total conservation environment for the whole of the collections in all kinds of library.   How-

ever, it is the important duty of librarians to be fully conscious of the damage that will result from conditions below these standards and in the light of this knowledge to establish priorities that ensure that the required conservation environment is accorded for the preservation of their collections for whatever period of time they judge to be necessary or possible.

2. 11   The implications of this are that a conscious attitude towards decisions about conservation should be applied to all library collections.   It may well be that a deliberate decision is made in some libraries that their collections need to survive for only a relatively short time, while in other libraries it may be decided that the whole collections must be given conditions in which they will survive as long as possible.   In many libraries it will be decided that a particular part of the collections must survive as long as possible and in this case suitable conservation conditions are best provided by the establishment of a special department (Rare book department, Reserve).

2. 12   Very frequent usage of library materials poses dangers of repeated handling and the use of items of value should whenever possible be restricted to those who really have need for access to originals.   Unique items and items of very special value should be protected against repeated usage. This can be achieved by preparing photographic copies for users who do not require the original.

2. 13   For the most important of such items there should be three complete photographic copies of each item: 1) a copy for regular usage, 2) a security copy to be preserved at a different place from the original, 3) a copy to be used for the making of further copies.

2. 14   This is, of course, an expensive undertaking for a library and has probably to be restricted to items of the very greatest importance.   The making of such security photographic copies may in some instances be properly regarded as a national responsibility.

2. 15   As another means of providing security for originals librarians should, when possible, encourage the production of facsimile editions.

2. 16   Items of especial value should be protected against excessive exposure in exhibitions and against the dangers of transport that arise from the inclusion of such items in exhibitions outside the library building and particularly in travelling exhibitions.

3.   Protection against physical damage

3. 1   It is the duty of librarians to ensure that adequate measures are taken to protect the collections in their care against physical damage.

3. 2   Unbound books are very exposed to physical damage; single sheets are even more exposed.   Some form of protection is needed.   Single sheets (if not put into a binding) should be stored either in a special storage system, or put inside a cover or box of some kind.   Covers and boxes should not be overfilled, nor should they contain sheets of widely differing size.   The sheets should not be rolled or folded and care should be taken in handling to avoid creases.

3. 3   Suitable materials should be used for bindings, covers and boxes to ensure that the covers themselves do not lead to chemical damage to their contents (see 5. 1. 6).

3. 4   Storage of bound items should be on suitable shelving, each shelf being slightly larger than the books stored on it and leaving space for air circulation.   Very large bound items should be stored horizontally on shelves, but sparingly.   Shelf stops should be of a design that cannot cause damage to the volumes.   Covers and boxes containing single sheets should not be stored on shelves, but in cupboards or drawers.

3. 5   To guarantee the protection of collections against dust a regular and sustained programme of cleaning should be maintained, undertaken with care and under supervision.   The cleaning programme should also include examination of collections to provide early warning of biological or chemical damage.

3. 6   Library collections are, of course, for use, so it is the duty of librarians to ensure that their collections are used in such a way that they are not subjected to damage.   There are particular risks in the photography and photocopying of items and these operations should be properly supervised and controlled.   During photography care is needed to avoid excessive light and heat; during photocopying it is important that suitable machines should be used that avoid damage and that do not require a large amount of handling, particularly in the copying of pages from very large volumes. Special care is needed in the handling of bound volumes during photocopying, to avoid undue pressure on the spine in an attempt to obtain a copy that includes text close to the sewing.   If there is any risk of damage volumes should not be photocopied and a photographic copy should be made.

3. 7   As library staff are in many instances the most frequent handlers of library materials, it is important that all library staff should receive training in their libraries on the safest methods of handling and transporting library materials of all kinds.

4.   Protection against biological damage

Biological agents (micro-organisms and insects) can cause serious and sometimes irreparable damage to library materials and to the wood fittings of libraries.

4. 1   Micro-organisms

4. 1. 1   Micro-organisms cause changes of colour in library materials (e. g. foxing) sometimes causing them to become fragile, and a very serious attack can destroy them.

4. 1. 2   The growth and reproduction of micro-organisms is assisted by certain physical and chemical factors: unsuitable environment (high temperature and humidity, overcrowded storage), dust and the presence in the books of substances (adhesives, glues, etc.) that are vulnerable to attack.

4. 1. 3   These physical and chemical factors need to be strictly controlled to provide protection against attack.

General guidance on climatic conditions is described in 2. 3-6, but specialist advice is needed on local optimal conditions for preventing the growth of micro-organisms.   The advice of relevant specialists is needed in the choice of suitable materials for restoration work, to avoid materials vulnerable to attack by micro-organisms.

4.1.4 If an infection by micro-organisms occurs, assistance from a microbiologist is needed to identify the factors that have led to their growth and to advise on the measures required to arrest the damage. When the nature and extent of the attack has been identified, specialist advice must be obtained and strictly followed on the choice of a suitable disinfectant and the mode of use (concentration, temperature, humidity and period of exposure) which will ensure that it is not only effective, but also harmless to the materials of the infected books (paper, vellum, wood, leather, inks and colours).

4.2 Insects

4.2.1 Insects cause not only in books themselves but also in the wood fittings of libraries erosions that have diverse but well defined morphological characteristics.

4.2.2 The growth of insects is assisted by the same factors as those described for micro-organisms (4.1.2).

4.2.3 To provide protection against attack the same measures need to be adopted as against micro-organisms (4.1.3).

4.2.4 If an infestation occurs, assistance from an entomologist must be obtained as a matter of extreme urgency to identify the infesting species and to advise on the most effective insecticide and its mode of use. However, additional specialist advice must be obtained and strictly followed to ensure that the treatment is harmless to the materials of the infested books.

5. Protection against chemical damage

The advice of a chemist experienced in library conservation should always be obtained before any treatment involving solvents or any other chemical is undertaken.

5.1 Chemical damage to paper

5.1.1 The two main causes of chemical damage to paper are oxidation and the hydrolysis of cellulose. In general library conservation it is not practical to take significant measures against oxidation, but a clear awareness of the nature of hydrolysis will provide guidance on the precautions that should be taken against it.

5.1.2 The hydrolysis of cellulose is the decomposition of cellulose under exposure to water (including normal air moisture). The hydrolysis is catalyzed by substances which are not themselves used up in the process. The most significant catalysts are acids of all kinds. Oxidation is catalyzed by heavy metals (iron, copper, etc.).

5.1.3 The warmer the temperature the faster both oxidation and hydrolysis accelerate, approximately doubling with every $10°$ C rise in temperature. Daily fluctuations in humidity and temperature may further increase the rate of degradation.

5.1.4 The acids that catalyze the hydrolysis arise from various sources: above all from cellulose processing and its by-products (e.g. lignin) and from additives used in paper production, from acid sizing (e.g. alum), from inks, printers' inks, colouring pigments and from atmospheric pollution.

5. 1. 5 To a large extent acids can be washed away; the harder the water used (i. e. the more carbonate it contains) the better.

5. 1. 6 A mildly alkaline buffer in the paper of a cover or folder serves as a protection against released or developing acids. Good quality and particularly old handmade paper contains such a buffer (calcium carbonate) as a result of the method of production. Whenever influence can be exerted upon production of paper, it should be insisted upon that it must contain no wood pulp and no more than traces of heavy metals (such as iron, copper) but should contain calcium carbonate. Calcium carbonate is the only buffer which from the evidence of old paper has been shown to work favourably under all circumstances with a content of 1% to 3%.

5. 1. 7 For the deacidification of paper advice from an experienced scientist should be obtained on the choice of the reagent and the procedure to be followed.

5. 2 Chemical damage to leather and parchment

5. 2. 1 Chemical damage to leather is mainly the result of improper tanning and/or atmospheric pollution. Storage conditions significantly affect the rate of deterioration of leather and parchment.

5. 2. 2 Deterioration of parchment is usually due to microbiological attack. Parchment is in general more resistant than leather to polluted atmosphere. When chemical damage occurs in parchment, it is usually caused by very unfavourable storage conditions and by unsuitable inks, sizing or other added materials.

5. 2. 3 Strict control of storage conditions, as outlined in 2. 3-7, is required for the conservation of both leather and parchment, since their deterioration is essentially irreversible and there is little available in the way of effective restoration treatment.

5. 2. 4 Some protection of leather against deterioration and damage is achieved by regular and systematic treatment with a suitable fat.

5. 3 Chemical damage to film

5. 3. 1 Film is especially endangered by chemical damage, as well as by physical damage. It must, therefore, be stored in containers of non-ferrous metal or other suitable material (e. g. polyester) that does not decompose to release any corrosive or oxydising substance. Unbuffered board, paper and wood are not suitable substances.

5. 3. 2 The best kind of film with a potential long life expectance is silver haloid film. If any influence can be exerted on the processing of film material, it should be insisted upon that the utmost care is taken in fixing and rinsing.

5. 3. 3 It is essential that film should be protected by storage in strictly controlled atmospheric conditions of low temperature and humidity with complete protection against air pollution and against light. The optimum temperatures to ensure conservation are $4°$ C for (old) nitrate film, $6°-12°$ C for (new) triacetate film, and below $0°$ C for colour film, with RH 20%-30%. These conditions must be provided if the highest level of film conservation is to be achieved. They are therefore essential conditions for security copies of the greatest value.

5. 3. 4   Film that is not stored in these optimum conditions will decay and
it is necessary to carry out a regular programme of recopying before physical or chemical damage becomes too extensive.   Collections of already
damaged film and prints should be copied without delay.

6.   General observations on restoration

6. 1   It is not possible to reverse the process of decay.   Restoration in the
absolute sense is therefore not possible.   The restoration of a decayed item
in a library collection is the stabilization and reconstruction of the decayed
and damaged object, using as much of the original material as is functionally possible but also new material where necessary.   This process always
means a change: some properties of the original materials will be preserved at the expense of others and it is for the librarian to decide whether
this change is acceptable or not.   The aim of restoration is to provide the
new restored object with as many of the qualities as possible, functional,
visual and tactile, as the original.

6. 2   Before restoration of an object is undertaken the librarian must assess,
with technical advice from conservation and restoration experts, whether
restoration is necessary, or whether the object can be suitably preserved
for its normal usage by taking appropriate conservation and protection measures.   Restoration should never be undertaken unless it is unavoidable.

6. 3   The need for any form of restoration implies that decay or damage has
already taken place on such a scale that the item can no longer be used.
Frequent use is in most cases a more compelling reason for undertaking
restoration than the level of decay or damage.   Books even in poor condition are in no great danger, at least in the short term, if they are out of
use and stored in good conservation conditions.

6. 4   To assist in deciding what restoration needs to be undertaken in a collection, an inventory needs to be compiled, even on a limited scale, and
regularly brought up to date so that the current condition of items in the
collection is recorded in detail.

6. 5   Restoration work on library collections is inherently an expensive process in labour, and sometimes also in materials.   As the aim is to make
an item fit for use as long as possible, the librarian may decide that the
needs of availability of the text may more economically be met by another
copy, or by a microfilm or photocopy, while the original is kept stable by
suitable storage out of usage.

6. 6   With the great quantity of items in need of restoration (especially in
older collections) and the wide variety in the possible methods of restoration, librarians must decide with the advice of their restoration experts
upon the type and degree of restoration that is necessary.   Before the decision is taken a detailed study of the structure of each book and of its materials must be made.   This will ensure that the most suitable methods and
materials are used.   It will also ensure that details that may be of historical interest are observed and recorded.

6. 7   Materials for restoration work (papers, leathers, tissues, adhesives,
etc.) and especially chemicals (solvents, bleaching agents, solutions for deacidification etc.) should be used only after advice on their use has been
obtained from a chemist with special knowledge of the material or chemical
and with experience of their use in restoration.

6. 8 All forms of restoration work on any item must be fully recorded, including in some cases photographic documentation.   A description (or photographs) of the state of the item before treatment and details of the treatment
(including the materials and chemicals used) are essential to provide complete evidence of the changes that restoration has introduced.   The item
should be clearly marked as having received restoration and the documentation on the restoration (showing when the treatment was undertaken and by
whom) should be kept readily available for consultation by users of the book.

7.   Restoration of the body of an item or of individual leaves

7. 1 The aim of the restoration should be to match or even surpass the
durability of the original.   It is, however, important that the visual and
tactile qualities of the object should be left as little changed as possible.

7. 2 In the choice of materials for restoration work and of the techniques
for their use, their suitability, durability, safety and (as far as possible)
the reversibility of the process should be the prime consideration.   The
conveniences of rapid and inexpensive treatment or the easy availability of
materials should be regarded as only secondary to these prime requirements.

7. 3 The librarian and the restorer need to be fully conscious of the dangers
of falsificiation and disfigurement during restoration.   This is particularly
necessary when considering the replacement of lost sections of illustration
or text.   Those replacements must be recorded with special care, especially
when they are not immediately identifiable.

8.   Restoration of bindings

8. 1 The purpose of the binding of a volume is to protect the body of the
book from damage and to delay the process of its decay.   It is therefore
inevitable that the bindings are themselves particularly susceptible to damage
and decay and many libraries have very large numbers of bindings requiring
treatment, repair or restoration.

8. 2 Restoration of bindings must be undertaken only if it is functionally
necessary (see 6. 2), for in many instances a box or slip case will provide
adequate protection.

8. 3 A library with a large collection of bindings requiring restoration
should consider the restoration not only of those bindings of exceptional
beauty and value, but of the collection as a whole.

8. 4 The restoration of a damaged or decayed binding should be undertaken
using as far as possible the materials and techniques of the original, as
long as the original materials or techniques provide a sound and durable
construction.   If the original materials are unsatisfactory or unobtainable,
a durable substitute as close as possible to the original should be used.
When making use of historical binding techniques and materials the restorer
should ensure that he recognizes their functions.

8. 5 If a binding is so severely damaged that it cannot be repaired but a
new one has to be made by making use of the old, all parts of it bearing
information of any kind (remnants of the decoration, marks of ownership,
old title and shelfmark labels, waste paper or vellum bearing text used in
the preparation of the binding) must be retained, even if their content and

value are not immediately recognisable.   All such details transferred to a
new binding should, if possible, be used in their original position and have
the same functions as in the original binding.   Care should be taken that
these original details are easily seen and sufficiently protected.   Alterations
which are not easily discernable (such as removed fragments) should be indicated in such a way that a user of the volume can identify them immediately.

8. 6 If only mere remnants of an original binding have survived, the librarian may decide that it is preferable to make a completely new functional
binding and preserve the remnants of the original separately.

8. 7 If nothing of an original binding has survived an unpretentious binding
should be provided that uses techniques and materials sympathetic with the
body of the book.

Reprinted from IFLA Journal 5(4):292-299, 1979, by permission.

GUIDELINES FOR YOUR LIBRARY BINDER

Because books differ in value and use, requirements for their rebinding also differ. Usually the most appropriate type of rebinding for books of permanent research value, that is, for books which have more than a limited short-term value but which do not have value as an object, is library binding. The following guidelines are meant to accompany the usual specifications given to the library binder.

These guidelines were drawn up with the needs of the majority of NEDCC clients in mind--New England town record offices, small historical societies, special collections departments and local history rooms in small public libraries. These guidelines are appropriate only when a relatively small amount of binding is being done (about a dozen or so volumes a year). Further, they are only appropriate for volumes which have signatures and are sewn through these signatures (i.e., volumes sewn-through-the-folds). These guidelines are not appropriate where a large volume of library binding is done annually (large research or large public libraries), or where the books needing binding are not limited to books sewn-through-the-folds but include books held together by other means as well.

These guidelines will cause the cost of binding to be higher than usual because of the extra time, handling and special attention necessitated by them. This higher price, however, is not usually prohibitive for institutions doing a small amount of binding.

When questioned informally, several library binders indicated that their firm could take measures such as these if requested to do so. However, some library binders prefer not to take any special measures and/or are unfamiliar with these measures, so you may have to search for a binder who is interested in this type of work. By an attempt to follow the guidelines the books will probably be treated with more care, a few of these measures will be followed, and the work produced will be more permanent as a result.

1) Do not trim edges of the book.

2) Do not cut spine of the book.

3) Retain original sewing of the book if possible. If not possible, re-sew the book by sewing through the folds.

4) In mending use paste rather than a white or animal glue. Use non-acid long fibered mending paper (Japanese tissues are preferred). Tear the tissue rather than cut it to avoid sharp edges against which the page could fracture when flexed.

5) Use materials which are chemically stable and durable throughout the binding process. Of greatest concern are the endpapers which come in direct contact with the first and last pages of the book. Endpapers should be acid-free or, preferably, slightly basic and buffered.

6) Save original covers, old labels, bookplates or anything else which might be of special interest even if saving this wasn't specified.

7) Call with questions about materials or procedures.

Reprinted by courtesy of the Northeast Document Conservation Center, Andover, Massachusetts.

Appendix C

ORGANIZATION FOR CONSERVATION

Appoint one person to plan and be responsible for conservation, preservation, and protection of all library and archival materials in, or to become part of, the collections. This conservator should:

1. Have authority to institute preventive conservation measures as necessary to arrest the deterioration of materials.

2. Assemble a library of conservation references including books, pamphlets, periodicals, catalogs and manufacturers' samples.

3. Conduct regular courses of instruction for staff personnel to keep them informed and up-to-date on preventive conservation practices.

4. Cooperate with staff personnel in the correction of unsatisfactory practices in regard to filing, shelving and long-term storage of materials.

5. Advise staff personnel on materials and practices suitable for the safe display of materials.

6. Monitor on a regular schedule the temperature, humidity, air pollution, natural and artificial lighting, housekeeping, and pest control and arrange for the correction of deficiencies when observed.

7. Prepare budget estimates for the conservation of the collections.

8. Plan an emergency and security policy and monitor equipment needed to safeguard holdings from fire and natural disasters and from theft and destruction by people.

9. Join conservation organizations, attend conservation conferences and cultivate the acquaintance of conservators, restorers, and chemists and physicists in laboratories involved in preservation research in order to keep current on conservation theory and techniques and guidance in specific problems.

10. Participate in available courses in conservation theory and preservation techniques in order to effectively supervise programs on the premises and coordinate the efforts of professional conservators under contract.

11. Cooperate with other libraries, museums and historical societies in solving common conservation problems and sharing technical information.

Reprinted by courtesy of the Northeast Document Conservation Center, Andover, Massachusetts.

Appendix D

RESEARCH CENTERS AND PROFESSIONAL ASSOCIATIONS

Appendix D in our Conservation of Library Materials [7263] listed some of the agencies available in 1972 to librarians and archivists seeking assistance in matters relating to the care and preservation of books and records. The following are additional activities in the United States, Canada and the United Kingdom, and some international establishments to which conservation managers can turn for help. Activities marked with an asterisk (*) have had address changes since the compilation of Conservation of Library Materials --Appendix D. Those wishing information on restoration workshops and conservations centers in other countries are referred to:

a) Bollettino dell'Istituto Centrale per la Patologia del Libro XIX Fasc. I-IV Gennaio - Decembre 1970 (pp. 201 ff) for Italian activities.

b) A list of workshops prepared by the IFLA Working Group on Preservation in 1974. Available from Dr. H. Bansa, Director; Buchrestaurierung Abteilung Bayerische; Staatsbibliothek, Ludwigstrasse 22; Munich 22, Federal Republic of Germany.

c) Preservãcao e Restauracão de Documentos: Lista preliminar de instituicoes. Rio di Janeiro: Biblioteca Nacional (ca. 1973).

d) Opportunities for Study in Hand Bookbinding and Related Crafts. New York: Guild of Book Workers, 1981 (pp. 18-21).

International

*International Center for the Preservation of Cultural Property (ICCROM)
Via di San Michele 13
00153 Rome, Italy
(formerly the Rome Centre, 256 Via Cavour, Rome).

*International Institute for Conservation
6 Buckingham Street
London, WC2N 6BA, England

International Federation of Library Associations
(IFLA) Working Group on Preservation
c/o Dr. H. Bansa, Director
Bayerische Staatsbibliothek
Munich, Federal Republic of Germany

International Council on Archives
Conservation and Restoration Committee
Dr. Lucio Lume, Secretary
Via Vaglia No. 11 (Nuova salario)
Rome, Italy

L'Association Internationale des Historiens du Papier (IPH)
Case Pastale   CH
4009 Basle, Switzerland

Canada

Canadian Conservation Institute
National Museums of Canada
1030 Innes Road
Ottawa, Ontario, Canada

Records Conservation Section
National Library of Canada and Public Archives of Canada
395 Wellington Street
Ottawa, Canada

Restoration Workshop
University of Western Ontario Libraries
London, Ontario

Restoration Workshop
Mills Memorial Library
McMaster University
Hamilton, Ontario

Pacific Conservation Center
325 Granville St.
Vancouver, B. C.

Canadian Group
International Institute for Conservation
Box / CP9195
Ottawa, Canada KIG 3T9

United States

The Abbey Newsletter
716 Gormley Drive
Rockville, MD 20850

The Albany Institute of History and Art
McKinney Library
Albany, NY 12210

*American Association for State and Local History
1400 8th Avenue, South
Nashville, TN 37203

American Historical Print Collectors Society
555 Fifth Avenue
New York, NY 10017

*American Institute for Conservation
1511 K Street, NW #725
Washington, D. C.   20005

Archival Conservation Center
8225 Daly Road
Cincinnati, Ohio   45231

Art Hazards Information Center
5 Beekman St.
New York, NY 10038

Balboa Art Conservation Center
P. O. Box 3755
San Diego, CA 92103

*William J. Barrow Research Laboratory
Richmond, VA
    (is no longer operating)

Bentley Historical Library
University of Michigan
Ann Arbor, MI 48105

Book Preservation Center
New York Botanical Garden
The Bronx
New York, NY

Book Testing Laboratory
Rochester Institute of Technology
Rochester, NY 14623

Bureau of Archives and History
New Jersey State Library
Trenton, NJ 08625

Clearinghouse for Paper Preservation and Restoration
New York State Library
Albany, NY 12224

Committee for the Preservation of Architectural Records (COPAR)
c/o Prints and Photographs Division
Library of Congress
Washington, D. C.

COPAR NEW YORK
c/o New York Chapter AIA
457 Madison Ave.
New York, NY 10022

COPAR Massachusetts
Post Office Box 129
Cambridge, MA 02142

Conservation Center for Art and Historic Artifacts
260 South Broad Street
Philadelphia, PA 19102

Conservation Department
University of California General Library
Berkeley, CA

Conservation and Bindery Department
University of Cincinnati
Cincinnati, Ohio 45231

Conservation Center
International Museum of Photography
George Eastman House
Rochester, NY

Document Reclamation Service
McDonnell Aircraft Company
Dept. 252, Bld. 102, MS 282
P. O. Box 516
St. Louis, MO 63166
   (Freeze Drying)

*Extra Bindery of the Lakeside Press
RR Donnelly & Sons Co.
Chicago
   (was closed in January 1982)

Georgia Department of Archives and History
330 Capitol Ave. SE
Atlanta, GA 30334

Graphic Arts Research Center
Rochester Institute of Technology
Rochester, NY 14623
   (All photographic problems)

Guild of Book Workers
663 Fifth Avenue
New York, NY 10022

Humanities Research Center
University of Texas
Austin, TX

Illinois Cooperative Conservation Program
Morris Library
Southern Illinois University
Carbondale, IL 62901

Kentucky Division of Archives and Records Management
P. O. Box 537
Frankfort, KY 40602

*Library Binding Institute
50 Congress St. (Suite 633)
Boston, MA 12109

National Fire Protection Association
470 Atlantic Avenue
Boston, MA 02210

*National Archives and Records Service Preservation Laboratory
Washington, D. C.
   (Was terminated in January 1982)

National Foundation for Environmental Control, Inc.
151 Tremont St.
Boston, MA 02111

National Technical Information Service
Port Royal Road
Springfield, VA
    (Clearinghouse for Federal scientific and technical information and
    some foreign material)

Nebraska State Historical Society Library
Lincoln, NE 68508

Northeast Document Conservation Center
Abbot Hall
School Street
Andover, MA 01810

Pacific Regional Conservation Center
Bishop Museum (P. O. Box 6037)
Honolulu, Hawaii 96818

Paper Services Division
United States Testing Company, Inc.
1415 Park Avenue
Hoboken, NJ 07030

The Preservation Laboratory and Bindery
The John Hay Library
Brown University
Providence, RI

Preservation Workshop
Marriott Library
University of Utah
Salt Lake City, Utah 84112

Preservation Workshop
Milton Eisenhower Library
John Hopkins University
Baltimore, MD 21218

Print Conservation Workshop
American Antiquarian Society
185 Salisbury Street
Worcester, MA 01609

Restoration Workshop
American Philosophical Society Library
105 South Fifth Street
Philadelphia, PA 19106

Rocky Mountain Regional Conservation Center
University of Denver
Denver, CO

School of Library Service
Columbia University
New York, NY 10027

The Society of American Archivists
330 S. Wells St. (Suite 810)
Chicago, IL 60606

North Carolina State Library
Department of Cultural Resources
109 East Jones St.
Raleigh, NC 27611

The Conservation Department
Stanford University Libraries
Stanford, CA 94305

Tennessee State Library and Archives
Nashville, TN

Thompson Conservation Laboratory
1417 NW Everett
Portland, OR 97209

Upper Midwest Conservation Asso.
Minneapolis Institute of Arts
2400 Third Avenue South
Minneapolis, MN 55404

Western Conservation Congress
10200 West 20th Ave.
Lakewood, Colorado   80215

Conservation Workshop
Yale University Library
New Haven, CT 06520

Great Britain

*The Bindery (British Library)
Great Russell St.
London

Bindery of the Library
University of Birmingham
Edgbaston, P.O. Box 363
Birmingham, England

Bindery of the Library
University College
London WC 1 England

*British Museum Research Laboratory
Russell Square London WC1B 3DG

The Secretary of the Library
The National Library of Scotland
Edinburgh, Scotland

H M Stationery Office Bindery
British Museum Great Russell
London, England

The India Office Preservation Center
Foreign and Commonwealth Office
197 Blackfriars Road
London SE 1, England

*The Institute of Paper Conservation
P. O. Box 17
London WC1N 2 PE
   (Formerly the IIC-UK Group)

The Leather Conservation Centre Ltd
c/o Mr. F. Jamieson
"Cloview," Ashlane, Martock
Somerset TA 12 6NP, England

Library Materials Research Group
Dept. of Mechanical Engineering
Imperial College of Science & Technology
Exhibition Road
London, England

Restoration Workshop
Department of Manuscripts
British Museum
Great Russell St.
London

Restoration Workshop
Department of Oriental Printed Books
British Library
Great Russell St.
London

Restoration Workshop
Lambeth Palace Library
London SE 1, England

Restoration Workshop
University College of North Wales Library
Bangor, Caernarvoushire LL 57 2DG Wales

Society of Designer Bookbinders
42 A Camden High St.
London NW1-OJH
   (Formerly the Guild of Contemporary Bookbinders)

Australia

Conservation Section
National Library of Australia
Canberra ACT 2600, Australia

The State Archives
2 Globe St. , The Rocks
Sydney 2000 Australia

New Zealand

    Conservation Department
    National Library of New Zealand
    Wellington, New Zealand

    Conservation Department
    Robert McDougal Art Gallery
    Christchurch, New Zealand

Appendix E

PAPER TREATMENTS

1. Surface Cleaning

Library and archival materials may be cleaned with brushes and cleaning pads in order to remove surface dirt, dust and grime. This dry cleaning technique may be used on book pages, manuscripts, maps and other documents. It should not be used on book bindings, book edges, intaglio prints (those with raised lines such as engravings, etchings, etc.), pastels, pencil, charcoal, watercolors, or other media which are not firmly bound to the paper or which might be lifted or erased by abrasives. Colors may smear, especially if hand applied. Art on paper should be left to the professional conservator.

Surface cleaning should precede wet cleaning and mending. If documents are not dry cleaned before washing, surface dirt may be ingrained in the paper. Adhesives used in mending can also set surface dirt in place.

Materials needed for dry cleaning are soft brushes and cleaning pads filled with vinyl granules (Opaline, Teledyne, Puffy, etc.) or canisters of vinyl granules (Skum-X, Opaline, etc.).

To begin work, clear an area that has a large, clean, smooth surface. It is most important to keep the work area free of the erasing crumbs produced by cleaning. Working on large sheets of brown Kraft paper may help you to dispose of the crumbs. If crumbs remain on the working surface and the paper to be cleaned is placed on them and rubbed, holes may be rubbed in the paper.

Begin the cleaning by brushing the surface of the object with a soft brush to remove loose dirt and dust. Use up and down strokes and work across the paper. Be careful to avoid tears by working towards the tears. With books, be sure to brush the dirt out of the gutter.

Use of a dry cleaning pad will remove more dirt than a brush. Knead the pad to release the crumbs. It is important to test in an inconspicuous spot before beginning work. Steady the paper with one hand and test by gently rubbing the pad in one area. Once it is certain that the medium is not being lifted or erased, start from the middle of the object and work towards the edges. A circular motion can be used, rubbing in small circles with the pad and systematically covering the entire surface. When cleaning near the edges do not use a circular motion, but rub from the middle towards the edges. This will prevent tearing the edges, which are often fragile, and ripping dog-eared corners. Be careful going over inks which have eaten through or weakened the paper. Avoid areas of color or pencil notations, which may be archivally significant. Complete removal of a pencil notation usually requires a harsher abrasive and an experienced hand.

Some people prefer to use their fingers for dry cleaning. Sprinkle granules from a canister over the object to be cleaned or knead granules out of a cleaning pad. Using your fingers, rub the granules gently over the surface of the object. Fingertips, rather than the pad, should be used in areas where the paper is torn.

Crumbs and loosened dirt produced during the cleaning process should be brushed away frequently. If the crumbs appear to have color other than dirt, check to make sure that ink or color is not being lifted from the document. Keep a careful eye on your work at all times to make sure that you are not erasing or lifting anything but surface dirt, and that you are not smearing the medium or producing any tears.

It is essential that all granules be removed from the object following cleaning. Brush both sides of the object thoroughly with a soft brush and make certain the work surface is free of granules. Give special attention to the gutters of books, where granules may accumulate. Remove treated objects from the work area.

While the granules of a dry cleaning pad or powder will remove most surface dirt, erasers may remove even more. However, it is not necessary, or even desirable, to remove all surface dirt from old documents. Erasers can abrade soft papers and are best used by persons experienced in surface cleaning. If it is necessary to use an abrasive harsher than Opaline or Skum-X, the Magic Rub eraser is comparatively safe. Proceed with caution, trying an inconspicuous spot first. Do not rub hard and take care not to create light erased areas which will contrast with the general surface color. Do not use erasers over pencil, color and inks.

2. Repairing Paper

The generally accepted method of repairing torn paper or reinforcing weak areas in a sheet is a wet method which involves patching with strips of strong, almost transparent acid-free paper. The strips are adhered with a sufficiently strong, colorless adhesive which is both acid-free and easily reversed. The following materials are used and recommended by paper conservators for repair of paper objects. They are used for hinging paper objects as well as mending and reinforcing.

Mulberry Paper:
The preferred acid-free repair paper is handmade in Japan from the inner bark of the paper mulberry tree. Mulberry papers (often erroneously called rice papers) exist in different weights with names such as Sekishu, Tengujo, Kizukishi and Usumino. The lighter weight papers especially Tengujo or Tosa are especially well suited to document repair since they are transparent and unobtrusive and will not obscure the text of the document. These papers are available from conservation suppliers. Some art supply stores also sell Japanese papers, but those tend to be poorer quality machine-made types. They resemble the handmade papers but lack permanence and strength. Handmade Japanese papers are ideal for repairs because they are strong, relatively transparent and composed of a high quality alpha cellulose which does not discolor or become brittle with time. Most conservators use torn strips of this paper because a frayed edge makes a less visible repair.

Adhesives:
Use of a proper adhesive is essential. Any adhesive used for mending paper objects must have the following properties:

* Sufficient strength to hold the object for an indefinite length of time--
  the adhesive must continue to hold as it ages;
* Permanent colorlessness--it should not yellow or darken or stain the
  paper;
* Reversibility--it must allow the repair paper to be easily removed
  with a minimal amount of moisture, even after many years.

Few commercially available adhesives meet all these criteria. Rubber cement, animal glues, or gelatin will inevitably darken or stain. Commercial library or wallpaper pastes may lose hold on aging and often contain harmful additives. There are several synthetic adhesives such as white glues which do not stain but which are very difficult if not impossible to remove.

The adhesives found on most "pressure sensitive" (self adhering) tapes will stain almost immediately and should be avoided at all costs. We know of one transparent self-sticking tape which is not supposed to discolor paper, but conservators do not recommend it because it is difficult for anyone other than a conservator to remove. The adhesives on commercial gummed tapes, which require wetting, are less damaging. But most, including the gummed linen tape favored by many framers for hinging may stain in time and should be avoided with objects of value. The glassine stamp hinge paper currently available does not cause staining but is neither strong nor aesthetically pleasing.

Commercial products in general should be avoided even if they appear "safe" because commercial products are subject to alteration by the manufacturer. This year's non-staining tape may have an adhesive with a different formula next year.

Most often recommended: Starch-based paste. For many years conservators have favored homemade starch-based pastes. These are made most often from either rice or wheat starch (not flour but the starch which has been extracted from the flour and which is available from conservation suppliers).

One recipe for wheat starch paste follows:

* Place one cup of wheat starch and five or six cups of water in the top
  of a very clean double boiler.
* Mix well and let stand at least 20 minutes.
* Fill bottom part of double boiler with a small amount of cold water so
  that the upper section does not touch the water.
* Place on medium high heat and cook, stirring constantly with a clean
  wire whisk.
* When the paste begins to thicken (this may happen right away), reduce
  heat and continue stirring.
* Stir for about half an hour; then remove from stove. The paste should
  be thick and translucent. As it cooks and thickens, it will become
  more difficult to stir. To aid in stirring, a wooden spoon may be
  substituted for the wire whisk, but the spoon should be one which has
  not been used in the preparation of food.
* When cooked, the paste should be strained through cheesecloth or a
  Japanese paste strainer (from conservation suppliers) and stored in a
  clean jar. It should be allowed to cool before use.
* On cooling, the paste may become thick and rubbery. If so, strain
  again prior to use and slowly mix with water until the paste reaches a
  workable consistency.

Conservators differ in their preference of how thin paste should be.   A consistency similar to heavy cream is adequate for mending.

This wheat starch paste should not be refrigerated.   Unless a preservative is added, it will keep for a week or less.   Some conservators recommend adding a few drops of eugenol as a preservative; we have found thymol gives longer lasting protection.   Thymol, bought in the form of pungent white crystals from chemical suppliers, is not soluble in water so must be dissolved in methyl alcohol (methanol) before being added to the paste. Take 5cc of methyl alcohol (about one teaspoon) and add thymol crystals to it until the solution is saturated; that is until the crystals no longer dissolve.   Add the thymol solution to freshly made paste while the latter is still hot and stir for several minutes.

With thymol added, paste will last for several weeks.   Do not refrigerate but store covered in a cool, dry place where there is no danger of mold contamination.   If paste discolors, grows mold or develops a sour smell, discard immediately.   Discard also if dark flecks appear in the paste as these may be the onset of mold or bacterial growth.

A Simpler Paste: Starch pastes do require time to make and thus are not practical if they are to be used only occasionally.   A simpler paste can be made by buying methyl cellulose from a conservation supplier. Methyl cellulose comes in powdered form and is mixed with water to the desired consistency.   Let stand for several hours before use.   It may thicken on standing but can be thinned again with water.   Methyl cellulose is not as strong as starch paste but should hold adequately if the document is not to be handled extensively or if it is to be encapsulated in polyester film. Methyl cellulose may be strengthened by addition of a small amount of Jade 403, a white polyvinyl emulsion adhesive available from conservation suppliers. This very strong material should not be used alone because it is extremely difficult to remove after setting.   When mixed with methyl cellulose, only a small amount should be used; one part to eight or nine.   Methyl cellulose with or without Jade 403 keeps well for several weeks and does not require a preservative.

Applying the Mending Strips: First apply starch or methyl cellulose paste to the strips of Japanese paper with a flat brush (about $\frac{1}{4}$ inch wide) before the paper strip is placed on the document.   Then lift the strip with tweezers and place over the tear.   If the document is one-sided, place it on the reverse.   The thinner types of mulberry paper tend to pull apart when wet with paste.   It is easiest to use short strips, not more than two inches long.   For longer tears, more than one short strip may be used, placed end to end.   It will take practice to manipulate the thin, wet mulberry paper repair strips.   Once in place, tamp the repair lightly with silicone release paper or polyester web (from conservation suppliers) or with waxed paper from a grocery store.   Then blot lightly with a small piece of blotting paper or paper toweling.   If possible, weight the repair while it dries.   Weighting insures good adhesion and prevents cockling of the paper.   Repairs may be weighted as follows: first place small pieces of blotting paper over and under the area to be dried.   A piece of glass is laid on top of the blotter and a weight (about one pound) on top of the glass. The weights may be small bags of lead shot or pieces of lead covered with cloth or cloth tape.   One pound fishing weights from sporting goods stores make excellent weights provided they have at least one flat side to prevent rolling.   Repairs should be weighted for one hour or longer.   Use of a small photographer's tacking iron can speed up the drying process greatly. This instrument should not be applied directly to the document.   Place a piece of thin blotter or moderately heavy absorbent paper between the iron and the document. Iron until apparently dry, then weight for a few minutes to encourage flatness.

Repairing with heat set tissue: In recent years some conservators have repaired tears with thin tissue paper impregnated with synthetic resins. This is applied by pressure and heat from a photographer's tacking iron, preferably on a Teflon coated surface.   The tissue to use is the one developed at the Library of Congress which is available from

August Velletri
Bookmakers
2025 Eye Street, N. W.
Room 307
Washington, DC 20006

The tissue is torn in thin 1/4" to 3/8" strips and laid over the tear shinyside down.   Weak areas may be reinforced if necessary with larger patches.   A thin piece of Japanese mulberry paper, silicone release paper or white polyester fabric must be placed over the mending strip between it and the iron.   The iron should be heated to 190-200° F.   Use of a heated platen press set at 180° F gives good results for mending or reinforcing large areas.   With a heated press the document should be sandwiched between release paper or polyester and pressed for at least eight seconds.

For small tear mends, hand pressure with the hot iron is usually sufficient to achieve consolidation.

The shape of the heat-set tissue patch must be carefully considered so as to be consistent with the nature and position of the tear and the general condition of the paper.   For mending lacunae, two patches slightly larger than, yet conforming to the contours of the missing area should be shaped in the following manner: Place a sheet of polyester film over the lacuna and place the tissue over the film.   With a dissecting needle, outline on the tissue the desired shape of the patch and tear along the line made with the needle.

A tear which leads in from an edge is best mended by tearing heat-set tissue so that it tapers from the inner area of the tear to the outer edge of the paper.

Ordinarily, heat set tissue is applied to the reverse side of a document.   If necessary to support both sides the two tissue patches must be of different sizes, one larger than the other.

Tinted heat-set tissue may be made for cases in which the whiteness of the lens tissue contrasts too starkly with the tone of the paper to be mended.   After the acrylic coating has dried on the lens tissue, brush the tissue side with a water color solution slightly lighter than the tone of the paper.   When heat is applied to tinted tissue, it tends to darken.

An alternative method for making the heat-set tissue a more sympathetic color in relation to the paper is to brush the tissue lightly with ethanol after the mend has been applied.

The advantage of using heat set tissue is that it is more quickly applied and does not require weighting after application. Heat set tissue is more expensive, however, and is less strong than Japanese paper. Heat set mends may not adhere as well. In general, conservators prefer repairs made of Japanese mulberry paper and a starch based adhesive.

3.   Nylon Gossamer Webb Reinforcement

Materials

1 ordinary household flat iron
2 sheets of silicone release paper
  about 2" larger on all 4 sides
  than the document to be backed.

1 sheet of Nylon Gossamer Webb
  reinforcement about 1" larger on
  all 4 sides than the document to
  be backed.

The document to be reinforced

A flat surface on which to work.

Silicone release paper available from: TALAS
                                          Division of Technical Library
                                            Services
                                          130 Fifth Avenue
                                          New York, New York 10011.

Nylon gossamer webb reinforcement
available from: Process Materials
                                          329 Veterans Boulevard
                                          Rutherford, New Jersey 07070
                                          or from TALAS.

Heat sensitive nylon webb
available from: Process Materials.

Document should be cleaned with soft erasers or opaline

Document to be reinforced should first be deacidified if this is necessary either through soda water process or Wei T'o spray deacidification or the Barrow process.

Cut two pieces of silicone
release paper about 1"
larger than the document.
Place one sheet on the table,
which should be flat.   The
silicone paper should be
cushioned by one or two
blotters

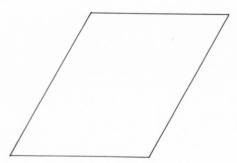

On the silicone paper place
the document to be reinforced
face down.

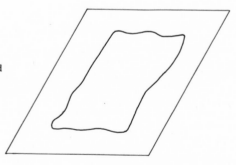

Over the document place 1
sheet of heat sensitive nylon
webb about 1" larger than the
document on all 4 sides.

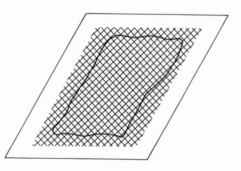

On top of the heat sensitive nylon webb place a sheet of Nylon gossamer webb reinforcement, the same size as the heat sensitive nylon webb sheet.

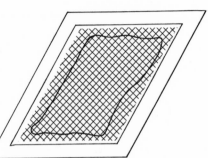

Finally, place the other piece of prepared silicone release paper on top of the nylon gossamer webb. Taking the flat iron, iron through the silicone release paper, moving the iron slowly and evenly outward from the center. The silicone paper can be removed and the document examined to see if the nylon reinforcement is adhering to every part of the document. If bubbles are discovered, replace the silicone paper and again iron through it until the reinforcement is adhering throughout.

Then the silicone release paper is removed from either side of the document and the document is placed under a slight uniform weight until the reinforced document has cooled. The document is then trimmed almost to the outer edge of the document.

4. Polyester Film Encapsulation

Encapsulation is a simple reinforcement technique designed to give added
support to paper documents and to protect them from physical wear and
tear. Documents are enclosed between two sheets of clear polyester film,
the edges of which are sealed with double-coated pressure sensitive tape.
The process is easily reversed by carefully cutting the polyester envelope
along the edges in the space between the tape and the object.

The condition of the object is not altered in any way by encapsulation. The polyester envelope primarily reinforces and protects the document. An encapsulated document can be safely handled by the general public, and may withstand even rough handling. Since the document is sealed
in a near vacuum, it is also protected in other ways: from pollutants,
from acid migration from adjacent materials and, to some extent, from
changes in temperature and relative humidity.

Polyester film is strong, flexible and chemically inert. If free of
plasticizers, U.V. inhibitors, colored dyes, and surface coatings, it will
not damage the paper it protects. Although many brands of polyester film
have proven suitable for conservation use, one which is readily available
is Mylar Type S which can be used in 3, 4 or 5 mil thicknesses. The tape
that should be used for joining the edges of the polyester sheets is 3M
Scotch Brand double-coated tape #415. This is the only such tape proven
stable during testing at the Library of Congress. Polyester film and
double-coated tape are available from conservation suppliers.

Encapsulated documents are held in place between the polyester film
by static electrical attraction. Static may help to hold fragile encapsulated
documents together, reducing the need to repair small tears before encapsulation. However, static in polyester film can also lift loosely bound
media from paper and makes encapsulation inappropriate for some pencil,
pastel and charcoal.

If a document can be so treated, washing or deacidification by one
qualified to do so is recommended prior to encapsulation. Encapsulation
does not halt the chemical deterioration of acidic paper, which will continue
inside the polyester envelope. However, documents may be encapsulated
without deacidification; they will benefit from the physical protection which
the method offers. Documents which are not deacidified prior to encapsulation should be so labeled for the information of future custodians. A label
typed on acid-free buffered paper, such as Permalife, and inserted inside
the polyester envelope with the document is more secure than one attached
to the outside of the envelope.

INSTRUCTIONS FOR POLYESTER FILM ENCAPSULATION

Materials Needed:

Scalpel, knife or small scissors
Lint-free cloth (cheesecloth)
1 Weight with clean felt bottom
1 Hard rubber brayer

1 Window-cleaning
  squeegee

Polyester film, pre-cut or in rolls: Mylar Type S or equivalent; 3 mil for small and medium size documents; 5 mil for large documents. Available from Transilwrap Corporation, 2741 North 4th Street, Philadelphia, PA 19133.

Scotch brand double coated tape #415, 1/4" or 3/8" wide. Available from Robert Spector, Inc., 46 Merrick Road, Rockville Center, New York 11570 or local 3M distributor.

A gridded work surface can be prepared by taping 1/4" graph paper to the underside of plexiglass or glass.

Instructions:

1. Cut two sheets of polyester film at least one inch larger than the document on all four sides.

2. Place one sheet of the polyester film on a flat hard work surface. Wipe the surface of the film with a lint-free cloth to remove dust and create a static charge, which will adhere the film to the work surface.

3. Center the document on the polyester film, leaving an adequate border for the double-coated tape.

4. Place a weight on the center of the document to keep it in position.

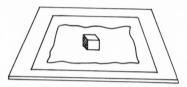

5. Apply the double-coated tape to the polyester film, leaving a 1/8" margin on each side of the document.   A graph paper grid placed beneath a glass work surface, will help to position the tape squarely.   The ends of the tape should be cut square and butted on three corners with no overlap.   A gap of at least 1/16" should be left at the fourth corner for air escape.   Leave the brown protective paper on the tape.

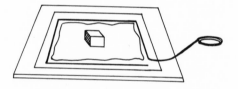

6. Wipe the second sheet of polyester film with cloth.

7. Remove the weight from the document and place the second polyester sheet cleaned side down on the document.

8. While holding the partially completed capsule down with one hand, use a squeegee to remove as much air as possible from between the sheets of film. Work from the center out to the edges.

9. Replace the weight on the center of the pack.

10. Lift one corner of the top sheet of polyester film. Carefully peel the brown protective paper from the tape on two sides of the document.

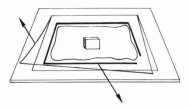

11. Repeat step ten on the diagonally opposed corner.

12. Use the squeegee to seal the tape and remove air from the envelope. Work towards the air gap left in one corner of the tape border.

13.   Roll the brayer over the tape to bond it firmly to the polyester.

14.   Trim the capsule, leaving a slight margin outside the tape on all four
      sides.   Rounding the four corners will help prevent scratching or cut-
      ting during handling.

Reprinted by courtesy of the Northeast Document Conservation Center,
Andover, Massachusetts.

Appendix F

PROTECTIVE BOXES AND WRAPPERS

1. American Philosophical Society Pamphlet Folder

The A. P. S. Storage Folder for storage of pamphlets, bound and disbound, and other flat paper objects.

To be made of acid-free material like Permalife Cover or Bristol.

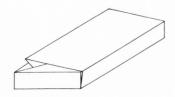

To enclose pamphlet in folder:

1. Crease all folds.
2. Lay pamphlet on Side 2.
3. Cover pamphlet by folding over Side 1.
4. Turn the whole onto Side 3.
5. Fold down Flaps A.
6. Cover with Side 4 and tuck Flap B under Flaps A.

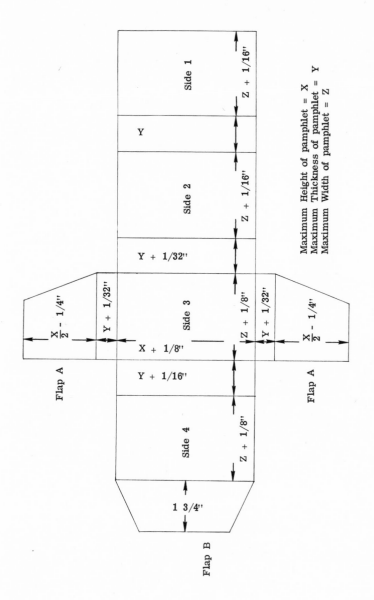

Maximum Height of pamphlet = X
Maximum Thickness of pamphlet = Y
Maximum Width of pamphlet = Z

2.   The A. P. S. Storage Folder (modified for book storage)

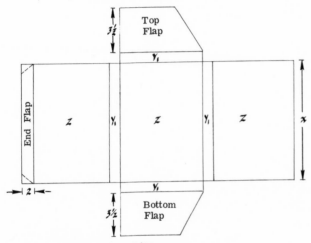

X = height of book + 1/8"
Y = maximum thickness of book + 3/32"
Y_1 = thickness of book + 1/16"
Z = width of book at widest part + 1/8"
Z_1 = width of book + 1/16"

The A. P. S. folder is made of a neutral, buffered folder stock--the light weight stock, 10 mil, is rigid enough to support a volume up to 3/8" thick, the heavier weight, 20 mil, will support a volume (or pamphlet or set of leaves) up to 3" thick.   For example, the A. P. S. now uses these folders to store contemporary typescripts on $8\frac{1}{2}$x11" paper.

        To make the folders, only the folder stock, equipment consisting of a mat knife, calipers, ruler and square, and ample working surface are needed.   A pair of sharp scissors can be substituted for the mat knife if necessary.   The most important requirement is careful measurement according to the formula shown with the diagram; the fractional additions are allowances for the thickness of the stock as the case folds over on itself.

        The folder was designed by Willman Spawn, conservator at the American Philosophical Society Library, in 1957 for the temporary storage of disbound pamphlets.

3.   Brown University Bindery Portfolio

Making a book and pamphlet portfolio

Object: to make a close fitting protective covering.

Materials: any acid free card or cover stock (depends on thickness of
                   book)
               Kraft paper tabs
               bias tape ribbon
               acid free paper for wrapping
               paste

Tools: ruler
               pencil
               scissors
               knife
               bone folder
               brush
               cheese cloth
               art eraser

Preparations: Bias tape--depending on the depth of the item being bound
cut six strips of bias tape into 7 to 10 inch lengths. If necessary the
strips should be cut longer.

        To make tabs--Cut 2" strips from the Kraft paper and then cut the
strips into 2" squares. The squares should be cut on the diagonal into two
triangles.

Procedure: The size of the paper should allow for the width and length of
both covers, the depth and length of spine and front edge and a flap at least
3/4 the width and two flaps at least 3/4 the length of the item to be bound.
See diag. 1 for parts of book.

        Working with the grain of the paper, transcribe the measurements
(working from left to right across the paper) of the:

    1. Width of front cover
    2. Depth of spine
    3. Width of back cover
    4. Depth of front edge
    5. Width of back flap

        Extend these measurements with a pencil line the full extent of the
paper. Starting from the top of the paper and working to the bottom,
transcribe the measurements of:

    1. One length flap
    2. The width of the spine
    3. The length of the front cover
    4. The width of the spine
    5. The other length flap

Extend these measurements with a pencil line the full extent of the paper.
The paper should have a grid appearance, see diag. 2.

With the scissors, remove the four corner rectangles of the paper cutting
along the inside lines, see diag. 2. Round the corners of the three rectangles which will ultimately be flaps, see diag. 3.

        With the bone folder and the ruler, score the remaining lines on the
paper, and fold the paper in at each line running the bone folder along the
outside of the fold to crease the paper.

BOOK
#1

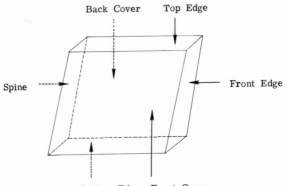

Back Cover   Top Edge

Spine

Front Edge

Bottom Edge   Front Cover

#2

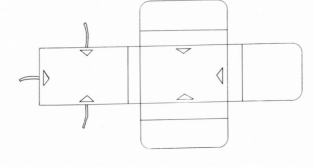

Top Flap

Front Cover   Back Cover   Back Flap

Bottom Flap

#3

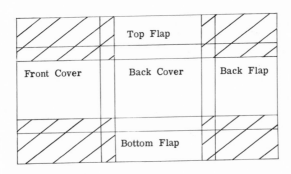

Take the knife and score a half inch long slit along the three outside edges of the front cover about 3/8 inch from the edge and midway between the corners. With the knife push through the slits to the other side of the paper. Repeat the same procedure on the back cover rectangle of the paper making sure the slits are opposite those on the front cover rectangle.

Feed the lengths of bias tapes through the slits in the paper leaving approximately 3/4 inch tape showing. Paste the ends of the tape to the paper. Apply paste to one side of the triangular tabs and cover the bias tape ends so that the longest side of the triangle is nearest the outer edge and the angle opposite the longest side points inward. See diag. 3.

Wipe away the excess paste with cheese cloth.

With the scissors snip off the free ends of the bias tape at an angle in order to keep the tape from fraying. All remaining pencil should be erased in order to present a neater portfolio.

If warranted, wrap the item in acid free paper in the same manner as a gift would be wrapped although no adhesive tape should be used to secure the paper.

Place the wrapped item onto the center rectangle of the paper keeping the front cover flap to the left. Fold the top and bottom flaps over first, followed by the back flap, and then complete the box by folding over the front flap. Tie each of the three sets of corresponding tapes into bows.

Judith B. Delmonico
Bindery Supervisor

4.   NEDCC Book Box: Design and Construction of Boxes
      for the Protection of Rare Books

Introduction

There is a growing realization among custodians of rare books and special collections, as well as among conservators, of the importance of preserving for as long as possible the complete bibliographical integrity of a given volume. A book is an object of several parts: textblock, binding, covering, and many subtleties of construction, all of which indicate provenance. These can be easily destroyed, yet each is significant to scholars interested in codicology or the history of the codex. Accompanying this realization is a changed attitude toward the conservation of such books, with less emphasis on restoration and rebinding (acceptable solutions when the textblock was regarded as having the most value), and more emphasis on the problems of total preservation. Such a change of emphasis creates challenges for both custodians and conservators, challenges which can be met only by a many-faceted preservation program.

Such a program should include (1) holding operations: low temperature storage and preservation boxing; (2) improved storage and handling operations: better control of the environment, better handling techniques, regular inspection, and minor refurbishing; and (3) restoration operations: cleaning, repairing, and rebinding. These last, more drastic treatments, usually become necessary because of failure to take proper preventive measures. As in so many instances, preventive measures are far more effective, and are certainly more economical and less destructive, than the

curative practices often resorted to after damage has already occurred.
The inescapable fact is that however carefully a restoration is executed,
there will always be a certain degree of bibliographic loss to the volume.
With many rare books, minor refurbishing and book boxes are, at present,
the only acceptable solutions for their preservation.

It has long been known that one of the most effective means of protecting rare books from physical and chemical damage is the use of custom-
made book boxes. In this connection, it is instructive to inspect collections
of books in which some volumes have been boxed while others have stood
on open shelving. One is immediately struck by the well-preserved condition of the volumes which have had the protection of boxes. Book boxes
protect the volumes by eliminating or reducing mechanical damage, such as
that caused by projections from adjacent volumes, by abrasion from shelf
surfaces and supports, by dust particles being ground into book surfaces
from friction, and by tugging at a volume held in tightly packed shelving.
Book boxes also minimize exposure to destructive environmental conditions
ranging from extreme fluctuations of temperature and humidity to pollutants
in the atmosphere. In fact, a custom-tailored box made of the best possible materials is the closest approach to a true panacea that is available
in the field of rare book preservation.

Many different designs of book boxes and containers have been used:
slip cases, telescopic cases, presentation boxes, Solander cases, drop-spine
boxes, etc. The choice of materials is also large: board, wood, cloth,
metal and synthetics. When designed for a particular purpose, boxes may
be made fire-retardant, waterproof, and/or specially adapted for traveling.

When large numbers of rare books need immediate individual protection, a long range preservation program divided up into steps or phases
must be initiated. The first step is action to arrest or retard the deterioration of a given collection, stabilizing it until funds and staff are available
for more extensive treatment. Within such a program, phased boxing, an
innovation developed at the Library of Congress, can provide temporary
storage at low cost.

The Library of Congress Phased Preservation Boxing Program

The first phased preservation program at L. C. was designed to save a collection of about 8,000 rare European law books dating chiefly from the 15th,
16th and 17th centuries, the majority of which were in unrestored, stiff-
board vellum bindings. This collection, subjected for many years to an
adverse environment (high temperatures and fluctuating humidity), had been
shelved in the conventional manner with no regard for size. Small volumes
were shelved next to large ones. Where the large volumes were free to
move, they expanded and contracted over the years in response to changes
in temperature and humidity, with severe damage to book structures and
bindings being the inevitable result. Other types of mechanical damage
were also widespread. Boxing was urgently needed to hold the volumes intact until actual conservation treatment could be undertaken, perhaps within
a decade or two.

The L. C. Phased Preservation Boxing Program was intended to accomplish the following specific purposes:

1. Retain all parts of damaged books.
2. Minimize further mechanical damage from handling.

3. Reduce further distortion of hygroscopic materials by the firm fit made possible by individualized tailoring.
4. Survey the collection for future conservation needs.

The "phased box" designed to accomplish the first three purposes is made in most cases from a single piece of card and tailored to the specific volume, fitting it snugly so as to restrict substantially any further movement of the structure in response to environmental changes.   The simplicity of the design permits the fabrication of large numbers of boxes quickly and at low cost.

Adoption of the phased preservation boxing program proposal and the box design itself depended upon acceptance by the custodial division concerned of the principle of reshelving in six size categories.   A second, indispensable accompaniment for this and other Phased Preservation Boxing Programs consists of an examination of each volume for specific historical features and for details of condition.   Observations are noted on a coded card, together with a small record photograph, in order to permit future recall of volumes with related characteristics or problems.   The phased box is most effective in valuable collections where the books need stabilizing but are not handled with any frequency.

Phased Preservation Box

Except for very large volumes a Phased Box Design is constructed from one continuous piece of board and is cut and creased to produce a base board, four walls and four flaps.   For both designs the tail flap is cut so that it extends approximately 1/3 over the book cover.   The other three flaps--spine, head and fore-edge--all extend to cover the full dimension of the book cover.   The head flap (1) is folded first to cover the dimension of the upper cover, followed by the tail flap (2), and the fore-edge flap (3) and the spine flap (4).   Thread ties and rivets will be attached later to flap 4. Thread ties wrap around the polyethylene buttons on the fore-edge wall and hold the book under tension within the phased box.

The listing of materials to be used in making these boxes follows.

BOARD: Any strong and acid free flexible board which can be creased without splitting.
BUTTONS: Circular plastic discs, 1" diameter x 1/16" thick.   Low density polyethylene is recommended because it is inert, has an agreeable stiffness and yet is flexible.   Punch holes in the center of the 1" plastic discs to accommodate the rivets.
RIVETS: Any small rivets (approximately 5/16" head) which, when attached, will hold the polyethylene buttons to the phased box board.   (At NEDCC thread is looped through a hole in the board and rivets are not used.)
THREAD: Any strong waxed thread cut to 9" lengths.

Regular Phased Box (One-Board Construction)

I. Measuring for the Phased Box Plan

Place the BOOK in the middle of the inside of the BOARD.   Roll the BOOK to the left and right and up and down to check that the BOARD is large

enough.   Place the BOOK in a position which will allow sufficient margins
for the flaps and place a weight on it.   Using an upright triangle, mark
the position of all outer edges of the BOOK on the BOARD.   Make a second
set of marks 1/16" to the outside.   This allows for clearance of the ridge
created by the crease.   (At NEDCC we find that measuring the extra 1/16"

BOARD MARKED AND CUT FOR REGULAR PHASED BOX DESIGN

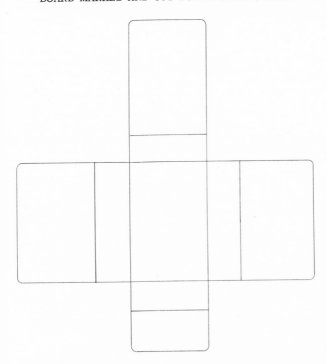

is not necessary when 2 ply board is used).   Working with a straight edge
and triangle, connect the second set of marks, making sure that all lines
are perpendicular and parallel.   See diagram 2.   This marks the BASE
BOARD area of the BOX.

A.   Determination of Height of Side Walls

Even though the BOOK is a similar height throughout, the walls of the
PHASED BOX vary because allowance must be made for the various flaps
that fold over and take up space.

Head Wall "A":   Height equals height of BOOK
Tail Wall "B":   Height equals height of BOOK plus 1 thickness
                          of BOARD
Fore-edge Wall "C":   Height equals height of BOOK plus 2 thicknesses
                          of BOARD

Spine Wall "D":   Height equals height of BOOK plus 3 thicknesses
                                   of BOARD

Mark these measurements on the BOARD and draw lines forming walls A,
B, C, & D. (Remember that the creases do take up a small amount of
space and allowance must be made for this.) See diagram 3.

> B. Determination of the Outer Limits of the Flaps
>   See diagram 4.

Flap #1:   Length equals length of BASE BOARD minus 1 thickness of
               BOARD
Flap #2:   Length equals 1/3 length of the BASE BOARD
Flap #3:   Width equals width of BASE BOARD minus 1 thickness of
               BOARD
Flap #4:   Width equals width of BASE BOARD

Mark these measurements on the BOARD and draw lines on which to cut.

II.   Cutting Out the Phased Box Plan
      See diagram 1.

With a leather hole punch (1/8" diameter) punch four holes at the corners
of the BASE BOARD.

Using a board-shears or a knife and a straight edge, cut all outside edges
of the Phased Box.

Round outside corners with a "round" chisel or corner punch (if desired).

III. Creasing on the Fold Lines

Transfer marks for fold lines on either side of the side walls A, B, C and
D to outside of BOARD. Crease the BOARD at these fold lines. Eight
creases are formed with the indentation made on the outside of the BOARD.
When folded inward, these creasing lines will disappear to form a rounded
edge on the outside. (At NEDCC we do not always transfer the marks, but
sometimes score the inside of the board and fold inward.)

IV. Attaching the Ties and the Buttons

The Phased Box is held together by two waxed thread ties which wrap around
the buttons on the outside. Two threads are riveted onto the fore-edge flap
4 approximately $1\frac{1}{2}$" from the edge at head and tail. (At NEDCC rivets are
not used. Thread is looped directly through the board. Buttons are sewn
onto the board with thread). Two plastic discs are riveted directly across
from the riveted ties in the center of side wall C. The waxed threads are
pulled over and wrapped around the buttons tightly closing the BOX. This
firmness restricts any distortion of the BOOK that can take place in varying
atmospheric conditions. See diagram 5.

> A.   Attaching the Ties

The Phased Box, now cut and creased, is placed face down with Flap 4 in
front of the box-maker. Two holes are punched at the fore-edge. The

MARKING BASE BOARD AREA
OF BOX

DETERMINATION OF HEIGHT
OF SIDE WALLS

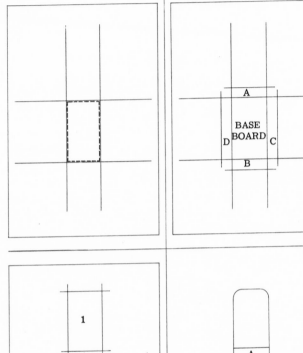

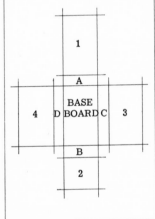

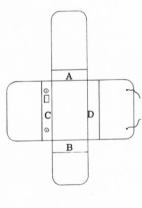

DETERMINATION OF OUTER
LIMITS OF FLATS

ATTACHING TIES AND
BUTTONS

placement of the holes depends on the size of the flap. A usual placement
is $1\frac{1}{2}$" from the head and the tail and 1" in from the fore-edge.

A simple half-hitch is formed in the thread and is placed over the male
part of the rivet.   The thread is drawn through the hole as the rivet is
placed on top and pushed together just to hold it in place.   The Phased
Box is 'hen turned over and the rivet is hammered together.   The short
end of the thread is cut away at the rivet.   Hammer on a firm surface--
the end grain of a square block of wood is ideal if the table or bench is
not firmly anchored.

B.   Attaching the Buttons

After both ties have been attached, the BOOK is placed in the Phased Box
and the flaps are folded over.   With the Box closed, the waxed thread is
drawn straight over the fore-edge and a pencil mark is placed in the center
of side wall board "C".   This indicates the placement for the plastic disc
button.   Remove the BOOK.

Working from the outside of the BOX, holes are punched at the pencil
marks.   The male part of the rivet is slipped under the board and put in
place in the hole.   On the outside, the disc is placed over the male rivet
and the female rivet is placed on top of that.   The rivet is hammered together.

The construction of the Regular Phased Box (One-Board Construction) is
now completed.   <u>See diagram 6.</u>

> --Design and Construction of Boxes
> for the Protection of Rare Books.
> Compiled and illustrated by Mar-
> garet Brown.   Library of Congress.

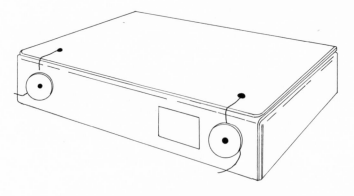

SOME SUPPLIERS OF MATERIALS

The list of suppliers in Conservation of Library Materials (Appendix G) is now only generally useful because of the number of company address changes over the years, and the new companies that have come into business in the last ten years. The following compendium of sources is offered as a convenient reference for most of the supplies and materials that would be needed for long- and short-range conservation programs.

Failure to list herein any supplier does not suggest that that firm is not reputable or that its products are not of good quality. There is just not room for all.

Art Supplies, Tools

Allcraft Tool & Supply Co., 100 Frank Road, Hicksville, L.I., N.Y.
    11801
516-433-1660

Art Mart, 1447 Second Street (Box 907), Plainfield, N.J. 07061
201-756-6868

Arthur Brown & Bros., Inc., 2 W. 46th Street, New York, N.Y.
212-575-5555

Brookstone Company, Brookstone Building, Dept. C, Peterborough,
    NH 03458
603-924-7181

Sam Flax, 118 8th Ave., New York, N.Y.
212-620-3000

Jensen Tools & Alloys, 1230 South Priest Rd., Tempe, Arizona 85281
602-968-6251

Environmental Monitoring Instruments

Abbeon, Cal. Inc., 123 Gray Avenue, Santa Barbara, CA 93101
805-966-0810

Applied Science Laboratory, 2216 Hull Street, Richmond, VA 23224
804-231-9386

Belfort Instrument Co., 1600 South Clinton Street, Baltimore, MD 21224
301-342-2626

Fisher Scientific Company, 711 Forbes Avenue, Pittsburgh, PA 15219
412-562-8300

Gulton Industries, Inc., Gulton Industrial Park, East Greenwich, R.I.
02818
401-884-6800

Psy-Chemical Research Corp., 36 West 20th Street, New York, N.Y.
10011

Science Associates, Inc., 230 Nassau Street, Princeton, N.J. 08540
609-924-4470

Climate Control

Bally Case & Cooler, Inc., Bally, Pennsylvania 19503. (Walk-in
coolers--refrigerated buildings)

Cargo Caire, Chestnut Street, Amesbury, Mass. 01913

Carrier Corp. (See local directory)

Fedders Air Conditioning & Heating System (See local directory)

The Trane Company (See local directory)

Equipment: General

W.O. Hickock Mfg. Company, 9th and Cumberland Streets, Harrisburg,
PA 18105
717-234-8041

Ernest Schaefer, Inc., 731 Lehigh Avenue, Union, N.J. 07083. (A good
source of supplies and equipment, new and used, including cutters.)
201-964-1280

Stacor Corporation, 285 Emmet Street, Newark, N.J. 07114. (Metal
map storage files)
201-242-6600

Fumigators

Vacudyne Corporation, 375 E. Joe Orr Road, Chicago Heights, Illinois
60411. (Non-portable equipment for large scale fumigation)
312-374-2200

H.W. Andersen Products, Inc., 45 East Main St., Oyster Bay, N.Y.
11711. (Ethylene oxide fumigation ampules and portable fumigation
equipment)

Healthio Medical, 250 Turnpike Street, Canton, Mass. (Ethylene oxide
ampules for portable units)

C.R. Bard, 731 Central Ave., Murray Hill, N.J. 07971. (Ethylene
oxide ampules for portable units)

General Library Supplies and Equipment

Bro Dart, 1609 Memorial Avenue, Williamsport, PA 17701
717-326-2461

Demco, Box 7488, Madison, Wisconsin 53707
608-241-1201

Fordham Equipment Co., 3308 Edson Avenue, Bronx, N.Y. 10458
212-379-7300

Gaylord Bros., Inc., Box 4901, Syracuse, N.Y. 13221

Highsmith, P.O. Box 25, Highway 106 E., Fort Atkinson, WI 53538
414-563-6356

Jostens, Library Services Division, 1301 Cliff Road, Burnsville, MN
55337
800-328-2980

General Supplies for Bookbinding

Andrews/Nelson/Whitehead, 31-10 48th Avenue, Long Island City, N.Y.
11101

Basic Crafts Company, 1201 Broadway, New York, N.Y. 10001

Gane Brothers & Lane Inc., Elk Grove Village, Chicago, Ill. 60607
(Graphic art equip. and supplies)
312-593-3360

Gentila Ferruccio, via Tiberina 116, 00100 Roma, Italy (Alum tawed
goatskins)

Harcourt Bindery, 9-11 Harcourt St., Boston, MA 02166

Harold's Eagle Works, Bedford, England (Leather)

Wm. J. McLauthlin & Co., Inc., 256-70 South 23rd Street, Box 7416,
Philadelphia, PA 19103
215-732-5823

La Pergamanta, Di Lui Lanfranco, 37060 Sorte di Chievo, Verona, Italy
(Parchment)

G.A. Roberts & Son Ltd., 2 Whites Grounds, Bermondsey SE1 London,
England (Leather)

Spink and Gaborc (Bookbinders), 32 West 18th Street, New York, N.Y.
10003 (Boxes)
212-255-8451

TALAS, 130 5th Ave., New York, N.Y. 10011
212-679-3516

J.S. Wesby and Sons, Portland St., Worcester, MA 01608 (Book cloth)
617-752-1984

For more complete information on bookbinding supplies, see The Guild of
Book Workers' Supply List 1979.

General Supplies for Conservation

Ademco Photo/Graphic, Ltd., 1000 Jay Street, P.O. Box 111A, Roches-
      ter, New York 14601 (Archival repair tape--laminating materials)
716-328-7800

Aiko's Art Materials Import, 714 North Wabash Ave., Chicago, IL
      60611
312-943-0795

Andrews/Nelson/Whitehead, 31-10 48th Ave., Long Island City, N.Y.
      11101
212-937-7100

Bookmakers (August Velletri), 2025 Eye Street, N.W. (Room 307),
      Washington, D.C. 20006
202-296-6613

Charrette Corporation, 31 Olympia Ave., Woburn, MA

Coastal Speciality Tapes, 274 Bangor St., Lindenhurst, N.Y. 11757
      (Scotch double coated tape #415--for mylar encapsulation)
516-226-5900

Conservation Materials, Ltd., Box 2884, 340 Freeport Blvd., Sparks,
      NV 89431
702-331-0582

Conservation Resources International, 1111 North Royal St., Alexandria,
      VA 22314
703-549-6610

Gallard-Schlesinger, 584 Mineola Avenue, Carle Place, L.I., N.Y.
      11514 (Chemical and laboratory supplies)

Gaylord now offers a limited range of conservation materials for libraries.

Gummed Tape Corporation, 147 West 15th St., New York, N.Y. 10011
      (Gummed linen tape)

Hollinger Corporation, P.O. Box 6185, 3810 South Four Mile Run Drive,
      Arlington, VA 22206
703-671-6600

E.T. Keeler Company, Wells, Chicago, IL 60614 ("Markilo" cellulose
      acetate document envelopes)
312-751-0047

Light Impressions, Box 3012, 731 Gould St., Rochester, N.Y. 14614
716-271-8960

Mail Order Plastics, 56 Lispenard St., New York, N.Y. 10013 (Plastic
      bottles and containers)

New York Central Supply Co., 62 Third Ave., New York, N.Y. 10003
212-473-7705

Panopticon, 187 Bay State Road, Boston, MA 02215
617-267-8929

Picreator Enterprises, 44 Park View Gardens, Hendon, London, NW4
2PN, England (Conservation and museum materials)

Pohlig Bros., Inc., P.O. Box 8069, Richmond, VA 23223
404-644-7824

Pratt-Spector, Inc., 46 Merrick Road, Rockville Center, N.Y. (Scotch
Double Coated Tape #415)

Process Materials, 301 Veterans Blvd., Rutherford, N.J. 07070
201-935-3900

S and W Framing Supplies, 1845 Highland Ave., New Hyde Park, N.Y.
11040

TALAS, 130 Fifth Ave., New York, N.Y. 10011
212-675-0718

Transilwrap Corporation, 2741 North 4th St., Philadelphia, PA (3 & 5
mil Type S Mylar)

University Products, P.O. Box 101, South Canal Street, Holyoke, MA
01041
413-532-9431

Paper and Paper Products

Aiko's Art Materials Import, 714 N. Wabash, Chicago, IL 60611 (Oriental papers)
312-443-0745

Andrew/Nelson/Whitehead, 31-10 48th Avenue, Long Island City, N.Y.
11103 (100% rag-content matboard, Japanese tissue, blotters)
212-937-7100

Art Mart, 1447 Second St. (Box 907), Plainfield, N.J. 07061
201-756-6868

Charles T. Bainbridge's Sons, 40 Eisenhower Drive, Paramus, N.J.
07652 (Mat and mounting board)

Hollinger Co., 3810 S. Four Mile Run, Arlington, VA 22206 (Acid-free
paper, boxes, folders)
703-671-6600

James River Paper Company, Tredegar Rd., Richmond, VA 23217
(Blotters)

Mohawk Paper Mills, Inc., 465 Saratoga, Cohoes, N.Y. 12047 (Specialty
products for the preservation and conservation of archival materials
--chiefly paper products)
518-237-1740

Washi No Mise, R.D. #2, Baltimore Pike, Kennitt Square, PA 19348
(Japanese paper and brushes)

S. D. Warren Company, Division of Scott Paper Co., Boston, MA 02101
617-423-7300

B. W. Wilson Paper Co., Britton Hill Rd., Richmond, VA 23230 (Acid-
    free paper, boxes, folders)
804-358-6715

University Products, Inc., P. O. Box 101, South Canal St., Holyoke, MA
    01040 (Acid-free folders, museum mounting board, rare book "Identa-
    Strips," other papers and card stock, cutters)
800-628-1912

Paper Lamination

Arbee Company, 6 Claremont Road, Bernardsville, N. J. 07924 (Lamina-
    tion, restoration of documents)
201-766-5534

W. J. Barrow Restoration Shop, Inc., State Library Building, 11th and
    Capitol Sts., Richmond, VA 23219
804-786-2310

Paper Testing

Applied Science Laboratory, Inc., 2216 Hull Street, Richmond, VA
    23224 (Makes and sells the W. J. Barrow Paper Test Kit)

Chicago Paper Testing Laboratory, Inc., Northbrook, IL 60062 (Paper
    testing facilities)
312-498-6400

Holland Library, Washington State University, Pullman, Washington 99163

Paper and Pulp Testing Laboratories, Fairfield, New Jersey

Paper Services Division, United States Testing Company, Inc., 1415
    Park Avenue, Hoboken, NJ 07030

pH Measuring Devices

The Barrow Test Kit is available from Applied Science Lab., Inc., 2216
    Hull St., Richmond, VA 23224 (Cost $20)
804-231-9386

Beckman Instruments, Inc., 2500 Harbor Blvd., Fullerton, CA 92634
714-871-4848

E. M. Laboratories, 500 Executive Blvd., Elmsford, N. Y. 10523
914-592-4660

Wei T'o Associates, Inc., 224 Early St., P. O. Box 352, Park Forest,
    IL 60466 (Also good for deacidification supplies)
312-748-2995

Ultraviolet Filtering Devices
(See the yellow pages in local telephone directories)

American Solar Tinting, Inc. , 6037 Liberty Road, Baltimore, MD 21207
301-944-0100

Cadillac Plastics, 134 Railroad Avenue Ext. , Albany, N. Y. 12205
518-459-3377

Colonial Kolonite Company, 2232 W. Armitage Ave. , Chicago, IL 60647
312-227-3400

3M Company, Industrial Tape Division, 3M Center, St. Paul, Minn.
55101
612-285-9600

Martin Processing, Inc. , P. O. Box 5068, Martinsville, VA 24112
703-629-1711

Rohm & Haas, Independence Mall West, Philadelphia, PA 19105 (Also
local Rohm & Haas distributors)
215-592-3000

Solar-Screen Inc. , 53-11 105 St. , Corona, N. Y. 11368
212-592-8222

Sun-X International, Inc. , 4125 Richmond Ave. , Houston, Texas 77027
713-869-8331

Transparent Glass Coatings Co. , Inc. , The Sun-Stop Building, 1959 So.
La Cienega Blvd. , Los Angeles, CA 90034
213-870-4777

Verd-A-Ray Corporation, 615 Front St. , Toledo, Ohio 43605
419-691-5751

ARTIFICIAL VS. NATURAL AGING OF PAPER

Table for determining the probable life expectancy of paper by artificially aging it at 100 degrees C in accordance with TAPPI T453 ts-63

Days of accelerated aging

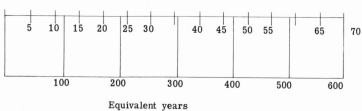

Equivalent years

Table from United States Patent 3, 898, 356
August 5, 1975 Williams, et al. "Method
of Deacidifying Paper"

SODA SIPHON DEACIDIFIER

Objective: To deposit magnesium carbonate in the paper to neutralize any acidity now present, and to neutralize any future acidity.

Problem: We would like to introduce the magnesium carbonate in an aqueous form. Magnesium carbonate has a very low solubility in water.

Solution: When water containing magnesium carbonate is charged with CO_2 the carbonate is converted to bicarbonate which is much more soluble in water. The conversion is greatest under pressure and at $4°$ C ($39.2°$ F). This bicarbonate solution can be applied to paper. When the paper dries in air the bicarbonate changes to carbonate.

Practical Application: A rechargeable soda siphon provides a quick, easy way to prepare small quantities of magnesium bicarbonate solution. We have had good results charging magnesium carbonate mixed in water using 10 grams of magnesium carbonate light power to each liter of cold water.

We are now using a Soda King Siphon which was purchased at a local department store. We have slightly modified the directions furnished by the manufacturer. The siphon has a capacity slightly less than 1 liter. We therefore mix 9 grams of magnesium carbonate in several hundred ml. of water. This mixture is poured into the siphon and the siphon is filled with water. We do not add ice. The bottle is assembled and the charger activated according to directions. Then the bottle is agitated for 5 minutes and put in the refrigerator for 20 minutes. It is removed from the refrigerator, shaken again for 5 minutes, and refrigerated again for 20 minutes. Finally, the siphon is agitated for 5 minutes and drained.

The solution should be covered, refrigerated and allowed to settle. The clear solution is decanted and used either as a bath, as a spray, or brushed on. Pre-washed (dry) items are soaked for 30 minutes, drained and allowed to air dry. A better alkaline reserve is probably obtained if the wet items are wrapped in polyethelene or aluminum foil and allowed to sit for 1 hour before they are air dried.

Note 1: Do not use this treatment on any water soluble inks or colors. A basic rule is always spot test with solution first.

Note 2: A transparent soda siphon bottle would be useful to determine the clearness of the solution. Such transparent bottles can be obtained.

Suppliers

>Magnesium Carbonate, light
>M-26 Lab grade
>Fisher Scientific
>
>Soda King Siphon
>Walter Kidde & Co., Inc.
>Belleville, New Jersey
>
>Soda King Super-Chargers
>Walter Kidde & Co., Inc.
>Belleville, New Jersey

Library of Congress Restoration Office.   November 1, 1973.

Appendix J

PRESSURE SENSITIVE TAPE SOLVENT

A) Dissolve 190 grams of Napthalene in one liter of Trichlorethylene.

B) When solution of the Napthalene is complete, pour the mixture of Napthalene and Trichlorethylene into two liters of Isopropyl Alcohol.

This solvent will soften and dissolve 90 percent of the adhesives found on pressure sensitive mending tapes that have been used in the past by well meaning but misinformed custodians of library and archival materials and works of art on paper.

CAUTION: Trichlorethylene is mildly toxic and alcohol is flammable; use only in a well ventilated work space (under a fume hood if possible).

Appendix K

FACTORS TO CONSIDER IN PREPARING DISASTER PLANS

1. Prepare a set of written guidelines for your particular facility in case of emergencies such as hurricanes, tornadoes, storms, floods and fires, and distribute to staff members. Consult Hilda Bohem's Disaster Prevention and Disaster Preparedness and Peter Waters' Procedures for Salvage of Water-Damaged Library Materials, in writing a disaster plan that suits your institution's needs.

2. For planning purposes assume that the worst might happen and services might be limited--no water, no electricity, no heat, no telephone.

3. Compile formulas and materials (such as formaldehyde, thymol) which might be needed for working with damaged books and secure the addresses and telephone numbers of suppliers of these items.

4. Prepare a checklist of tasks to be performed before an approaching emergency and choose the most observant and stubborn staff member for making the final check before leaving the building.

5. Include in this checklist such considerations as removing loose objects from near glassed areas if there is danger that these objects might become destructive missiles or might damage themselves. Also include the removal of paper and/or wooden items from on or near the floor to prevent saturation damage.

6. The card catalog in the average library probably houses the most expensive replacement ratio per cubic inch of any item in a library. It should be wrapped in heavy grade plastic and securely strapped or tied.

7. Compile a list of the location of all staff members during and following any anticipated emergency in case rapid contact becomes necessary.

8. Develop a list of contact people in agencies which can offer support after emergencies (with addresses and telephone numbers of contact people). Include firms which could supply or contribute materials and location of food freezer firms and refrigeration trucking firms.

9. In case disaster does occur consider an adjusted administrative structure related to restoration requirements.

10. Periodic if not regular staff meetings should be maintained for the purpose of evaluation of procedures, re-establishment of priorities and maintenance of good morale.

11. If any persons unknown to the staff assist in the restoration process, care should be taken to assure the staff who these people are, why they are present and how they relate to regular employees.

12. If a disaster is experienced make extra efforts to secure special cov-
     erage through news media in order to utilize public sympathy.   High
     level interest will normally be available only until the next major
     disaster occurs somewhere about the country.

13. Whenever offers of help do come, have available a list of specific
     tasks or materials which can be fitted to the person or establishment
     offering help.   Requests of a general nature often go unheeded.

This list now endorsed by the Northeast Document Conservation Center was
originally prepared by Dr. Carl C. Wrotenbery, Dean of Students, University of Corpus Christi, based on his experiences as coordinator of the salvage operations after the college's library was devastated by Hurricane
Celia in 1970.

TESTING FOR MAGNESIUM CARBONATE CONCENTRATION

The apparatus needed for this titration test is the Taylor Total Hardness Set, Code 1123, purchased from: Taylor Chemicals, Inc., 7300 York Road, Baltimore, Maryland 21204. In addition to the materials supplied in the kit you will need:

#1 filter paper, or S & S folded filters (#588 Fisher)
a 2 ml. transfer pipette
distilled water
2 small glass or plastic beakers

Directions

1. Place a small sample of the solution to be tested in one of the small beakers, and filter approximately 40 ml. through a cone of #1 filter paper, into the other small beaker.

2. Fill the 2 ml. pipette with the filtered liquid and then allow this liquid to drain off into the sink, thus rinsing the pipette with the solution to be tested.

3. Refill the 2 ml. pipette exactly, so that the bottom of the meniscus is at the 2 ml. mark, and drain into the 200 ml. Erlenmeyer flask. Hold the end of the pipette against the wall of the flask until the flow stops, but do not blow out the last drop as it is intended to remain in the pipette.

4. Immediately rinse the pipette with distilled water so that no magnesium ions will have a chance to affix themselves to the inside of the pipette.

5. In the 50 ml. graduate cylinder, measure out 48 ml. of distilled water. Exactness is not essential here, as long as there is at least 48 ml. Add the 48 ml. distilled water to the 2 ml. sample in the Erlenmeyer flask and swirl.

6. To the above add approximately 0.5 ml., or 10 drops of the Taylor Hardness Buffer and swirl.

7. Add 1 dipper of hardness indicator powder and swirl until dissolved. A light red color will appear.

8. Titrate slowly with the Taylor Hardness Reagent (EDTA) until the endpoint is reached, and the indicator changes to sky blue. While titrating swirl continuously. If done properly this test is extremely sensitive; one drop of the titrant is sufficient to change the color from pink to blue.

Note: The Barrow Lab suggests a result of 25 (25 ml. of titrant) for spray deacidification solution made up of 4 oz. magnesium carbonate and 1 gallon of water.

We have established a standard test result of 18-20 for solutions prepared in the soda siphon.   These solutions are used for disassembled book pages, or for brushing on to one side of a sheet for works of art on paper.

Library of Congress Restoration Office, November 1, 1973.

Appendix M

DISASTER PREVENTION AND CONTROL SUGGESTIONS

A Select Bibliography by Richard Strassberg

BIBLIOGRAPHIES

Cunha, George Martin and Dorothy Grant Cunha. Conservation of Library
    Materials: A Manual and Bibliography on the Care, Repair, and Restor-
    ation of Library Materials. Metuchen, N. J.: Scarecrow Press, 1971.
The bibliography, volume II, includes an eight-page section entitled "when
disaster strikes."

Evans, Frank, Compiler. Modern Archives and Manuscripts: A Select
    Bibliography. Society of American Archivists, 1975.
See especially section 10. 7 on "Fire and Water Damage, and Rehabilitation. "

International Institute for the Conservation of Historic and Artistic Works.
    Abstracts of the Technical Literature on Archaeology and Fine Arts.
    London, IICHAW.
The best up-to-date international bibliography. Issued periodically, it has
a separate section for paper. The abstracts are occasionally critical.

"Writings on Archives, Historical Manuscripts, and Current Records. "
    American Archivist.
Appears periodically and is a useful update of Evans.

PREVENTIVE MEDICINE

Banks, Paul N. "Environmental Standards for Storage of Books and Manu-
    scripts. " Library Journal (February 1, 1974), pp. 339-343.
Optimum standards for traditional library materials.

British Standards Institution. Recommendations for the Storage and Exhibi-
    tion of Archival Documents. London: British Standards Institution, 1977,
    11 p. ISBN: 0 580 09651 3
An excellent set of standards which cover everything from the site of the
facility to the kind of paper clips to be used.

Cornell University Libraries. Emergency Manual. Ithaca, NY, C. U. L.,
    1976.

General Services Administration. Protecting Federal Records Centers and
    Archives from Fire. Washington, GSA, 1977. USGD #022-602-000 49. 0
Useful scientific study.

Meneray, Wilber Eugene. Tulane University Disaster Plan. New Orleans, 1977.

Morris, John. Managing the Library Fire Risk. Berkeley: University of California Office of Insurance and Risk Management, 1975.

National Fire Protection Association. Archives and Records Centers. Boston: NFPA, 1972. 26 pp. (NFPA 232)
Includes building specifications.

_____. Protection of Library Collections. Boston: NFPA, 1970. (NFPA 910)
Among the least useful of this series.

_____. Protection of Records. Boston: NFPA, 1970. 92 p. (NFPA 232)
Includes specifications for fire resistive vaults, file rooms, safes and containers. Also vital records protection advice.

FOLLOWING THE DISASTER

Cunha, George Martin and Dorothy Grant Cunha. Conservation of Library Materials: A Manual and Bibliography on the Care, Repair, and Restoration of Library Materials. Metuchen, N.J.: Scarecrow Press, 1971. Volume I, Section on disaster recovery.

_____. "A Mobile Vacuum Fumigator for New England." Bulletin, American Institute for the Conservation of Historic and Artistic Works (AIC) 14:2 (1974) pp. 65-68.

National Fire Protection Association. Salvaging Operations. Boston: NFPA, 1964. (NFPA 604) 15 p.
Good practical advice written with fire departments in mind.

Pennsylvania Historical and Museum Commission. After Agnes: A Report on Flood Recovery Assistance... by Harry E. Whipkey. Harrisburg, 1973.

Spawn, Willman. "After the Water Comes." PLA Bulletin (Nov. 1973), pp. 243-251.
Good practical advice from a well-known conservator.

Waters, Peter, et al. "Does Freeze Drying Save Water Soaked Books or Doesn't It? Salvaging a Few 'Facts' from a Flood of (Alleged) Misinformation." American Libraries 6 (July-August, 1975). pp. 422-423.

_____. Procedures for Salvage of Water Damaged Library Materials. Washington: Library of Congress, 1975. 30 p. Free upon request.
From personal experience, the compiler of this bibliography can testify this is the best practical source on the subject. Store in a fire resistant safe above the flood line.

Appendix N

SUMMARY OF D. B. McKEON's DELPHI STUDY

Conservation of Library/Archive Materials: 1981-2001

The following predictions are the results of a detailed survey conducted as part of a PhD program in 1980-81, among conservators, conservation administrators, library school faculty members regarded by their deans as knowledgeable in conservation, as well as others active in the field.   The groups were surveyed separately, but their responses indicated no significant differences in their predictions.   Offered the chance to revise their views, virtually none chose to adopt the average view.

PREDICTIONS

The period 1981-2001 will be a period of economic stringency, overshadowing even the shortage of trained conservation personnel and the increased difficulty in the area of controlling environments.   National governments will continue to bear some of the responsibility for conservation of the cultural heritage.

Books and photographs produced after 1880 will be seen as in greater danger and will receive priority in treatment.   Despite the advances in reprography, originals will be still retained.

Outside centres will most often be made use of for conservation, with microfilming and mass deacidification employed for the preservation of materials.   Industrially organized library binders may become important in the restoration field.

It is unclear whether conservation will concentrate on simpler technologies with more manual operations or sophisticated technologies requiring fewer hands.

Except for a predicted reliance on external facilities and distrust of committing library and archives materials to courses which are irreversible, the technologies to be used are not at all clear.

Custodians will retain their traditional role of choosing materials to be preserved and in what order, but there will be some movement to involve them in responsibility for specifying technical processes.

Conservation administrators will usually no longer have been bench conservators.   Library schools will offer conservation courses, stressing developing conservation consciousness and familiarity with effects of different treatments.   A wide knowledge of the field will be more important than manual skills.

For these courses, faculty members will need to be trained conservators and a new training facility will be established in connection with some existing institution. Its student body will consist of science graduates and library personnel. Graduates will receive the certificate or degree for entrance into the conservation community. Informal acceptance will not suffice in the future.

Some inconsistencies are evident for the future: trained conservators will be wanted to teach librarians and archivists, but library schools will produce only administrators; librarians will learn technology and avoid making technical decisions.

"Now we see through a glass darkly, but then...."